Günter Gerngross
Herbert Puchta
Scott Thornbury

Teaching Grammar
Creatively

D1555928

HELBLING
LANGUAGES

Acknowledgements

Thanks to
- Jane Arnold for providing a shady tree, intellectual challenge and the right atmosphere for a key discussion in Seville without which this book probably would have never been written. Thank you, Jane!
- Mario Rinvolucri for his comments at an early stage of the previous manuscript for this book, and for being a friend and mentor for many years whose ideas have frequently brought new perspectives and insights into our work.
- Earl W. Stevick, whose books have had a lot of influence on our work.
- Robert Dilts for what he taught us about creativity and the mental strategies of outstanding people. (See bibliography for details of published work.)
- A number of colleagues for their support and comments: Tessa Woodward, Rick Cooper, Nathalie Hess, Adrian Underhill and Judy Baker.
- Seth Lindstroemberg for his editorial work, and Caroline Petherick for proofreading.
- Lucia Astuti and Markus Spielmann from Helbling Languages for their encouragement and support.

Günter Gerngross   Herbert Puchta   Scott Thornbury

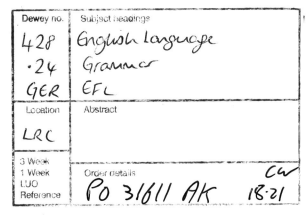

Dewey no.	Subject headings	
428 .24 GER	English Language Grammar EFL	
Location LRC	Abstract	
3 Week 1 Week LUO Reference	Order details PO 31611 AK	CW 18·21

Teaching Grammar Creatively
by Günter Gerngross, Herbert Puchta, Scott Thornbury
© HELBLING LANGUAGES 2006
www.helblinglanguages.com

First published 2006
Reprinted 2007
ISBN 978-3-902504-29-6

Edited by Seth Lindstromberg
Designed by Gabby Design
Cover by Capolinea
Illustrated by Piet Lüthi

Printed by Athesia

Every effort has been made to trace the owners of any copyright material in this book. If notified, the publisher will be pleased to rectify any errors or omissions.

Contents

Contents

Introduction

OVERVIEW

This is a practical book. It offers you a variety of lessons and activities for everyday use in your foreign language classes. Our aim is to stimulate the imagination, humour and creativity of your learners. The language structures we focus on in this collection are ones which our research into classroom practice and feedback from teachers of various nationalities have shown to be particularly difficult to get across successfully. We have not attempted to cover all possible grammar points. But we have tried to include a wide range of techniques which you can draw on when teaching grammar points not covered here.

The 53 grammar lessons that form the core of the book are each divided into two main sections: *Language Awareness Activities* and *Creative Grammar Practice*. The *Language Awareness Activities* are designed to introduce and provide initial practice of items that may still be unfamiliar to your students. The *Creative Grammar Practice* section provides an opportunity for a deeper and more meaningful acquaintance with these items, always in an extended context, and always with an element of individual creativity. Each of these two sections is self-standing: if your students are already familiar with a particular item, you can go straight to the *Creative Grammar Practice* stage. If, on the other hand, you want to provide them with just the first contact with a new area of grammar, without an elaborate creative stage, the relevant *Language Awareness Activity* can be done as a self-contained lesson.

We hope that both you and your students will find that grammar teaching does not have to be dull. We think that once you become familiar with the ideas behind these lessons, you will find it natural to adapt them to your and your learners' needs and you will discover that grammar learning can be fun.

RULES, FEELINGS OR CHUNKS?

Many adult learners have a very strong need to understand the rules by which grammatical structures are formed. They also frequently insist on being given rules about how and when a certain bit of language is used. For these learners, teaching with reference to explicit rules has definite advantages. There is practically no evidence, however, that the same is true for *all* adult learners, or for children and teenagers. Young learners especially (and some adults too) seem to be more at ease with holistic methods of learning grammar in which structures are acquired subconsciously. Additionally, there are mountains of evidence that many learners, of whatever age or tendency in learning style, are unable to transfer good formal knowledge of grammar to effective use. Such discrepancy between knowledge and putting it to use has led us to look for alternative ways of helping teachers to manage the practice of grammar in a more efficient way.

Earl Stevick's research has encouraged us in our search. Stevick (1989) analyses the widely varying strategies used by seven excellent language learners. One of these, Ed, is a highly successful learner who draws on three resources when speaking or writing:
- explicit rules
- remembered sentences and sentence fragments
- feelings derived from 'experiences about how a change at one point in a sentence will require a change somewhere else'. That is, instincts about regularities or patterns.

Stevick concludes:
All these kinds of resources are linked to one another, and so they help to retain one another in Ed's memory. The good thing about regularities and remembered fragments is that they operate more quickly than rules. (p. 94.)

Henry Widdowson has summed up additional evidence from recent studies:
Traditionally, second language pedagogy has assumed that the main difficulty for the learner lies in the acquisition of syntax. Learn the sentence patterns and then slot the words in. But so many words just do not fit. Learn the rules and then apply them. But the problem is to know when and where they apply. There are bound to be some exceptions. But there seem to be so many. Indeed the whole language seems to consist not so much of well regulated generative mechanisms as lexical chunks of varying size and variable syntactic adaptability. (From a talk at the ELT Conference in Vienna in 1989.)

There is thus a significant body of opinion that for some learners what is needed is the learning and recollection of bits of text exemplifying useful 'sentence patterns' and word or phrase use. Our experience is that such learners are in the majority, certainly among the young. Our book is designed to help you teach grammar to this common kind of learner, as well as to learners who are predisposed to learning through rules.

LEARNING GRAMMAR AS AWARENESS-RAISING
There's an English saying that goes "You can lead a horse to water but you can't make it drink". The same could be said about teaching grammar: you can teach the students the rules but you can't make them learn them. There are many reasons for this. The students may simply not understand the rules – this is especially the case for younger learners. But even adult learners have trouble with terms like *past participle, third conditional, inseparable transitive phrasal verb,* and with concepts like *indefinite past time* or *future in the past.* Also, research suggests that the learning of some grammatical structures follows a predetermined order so the fact that students seem to "resist" learning grammar may simply be due to the fact that they are not ready yet. Finally, teachers need to take account of the time lag between *understanding* grammar structures, and being able to *produce* them accurately. Some researchers claim that understanding is not only a necessary precondition for production, but that it often precedes production by a considerable length of time.

For all these reasons, many teachers now refer to the initial stages of grammar learning as *awareness raising.* Awareness raising is what happens when the current state of the learner's grammar knowledge re-organises itself in response to new discoveries. Unlike traditional (teacher-led) *presentation,* awareness raising is essentially learner-led. The teacher can provide optimal conditions for awareness raising, but only the learner can "discover" the grammar. This is why we refer to this first stage as *Discovery.* Typical discovery processes include *induction,* where learners are given some language data (such as examples of the target grammar item in context) and are then encouraged to work out the rules themselves.

LEARNING GRAMMAR AND THE HUMAN BRAIN
In his book *Righting the Educational Conveyor Belt* (1989), Michael Grinder reviews the ties between age, brain hemispheres and preferences in learning styles. He concludes that some people process, store and recall information more easily if it is presented visually, while others prefer auditory or kinaesthetic (movement and

touch) modes. The clear message here is that teachers need to know how to balance their reliance on visual, auditory and kinaesthetic input modes if they are to cater successfully for individual learning styles within a group. One of our major concerns has been to show ways of providing such balance.

Stevick (1989, p. 126) suggests that content and emotional depth of experience are also crucial factors in the acquisition of grammar. In other words, when it comes to teaching the genitive 's, a sentence like Martin Luther King's 'I want to be the white man's brother not his brother-in-law' will be better and longer remembered than 'The man's hat is green'. Accordingly, we have tried to incorporate into our model texts as much wit, metaphor, humour, fancy, absurdity and other imaginative devices as possible. The aim in doing this is to make these texts, and the language in them, as memorable as possible. Additionally – we believe – if the model texts are memorable, the corresponding student texts and the target language they include are more likely to be memorable too. Without memory, of course, there can be no learning. Accordingly, besides trying to provide examples of memorable content, we have attempted to include as many memory enhancing activities of all kinds as we could. (See, for example, 'Anchoring' on p. 11.)

FINDING YOUR LESSON

Suppose you need a lesson to practise *if*-sentences. How do you proceed? First, look in the quick-reference guide under *if*. You will see that there are four lessons to choose from (lessons 4.1, 4.3, 4.5 and 4.10). One by one, look these lessons up and decide which is best for your class. Then read the one you have chosen more carefully to see whether you need to adapt it in any way. Often, our lesson recipes include alternatives at various stages. However, there is another source of ideas for adapting a lesson at a given stage. For example, if you feel you need a different approach to the initial awareness-raising stage, look at the *Discovery* stage in some of the other lessons. Or, if you need a different technique or task-type at the *Text creation* stage, look at the *Text creation* stages in a few other recipes – even ones on quite different teaching points. You are bound to come across a range of different ways of proceeding. Finally, the Basic Techniques section (p. 9) offers a range of general options applicable to every lesson and it may well include something to help you adapt a lesson you have chosen.

THE STAGES OF THE LANGUAGE AWARENESS LESSONS

The *Language Awareness* lessons are each divided into three sections: *Discovery, Consolidation,* and *Use.* This three-way division may seem to reflect the traditional PPP format, ie, *Presentation, Practice,* and *Production.* In fact, there are good reasons for rejecting these terms. As we say above, the term *presentation* implies that learners learn precisely what teachers teach (or present to) them. In fact, learning is much less mechanistic and much more learner-directed than this older model suggests.

Likewise, traditional *Practice* activities always involve the learners speaking – often simply repeating – the new grammar structure. There is good evidence to suggest that forcing learners to speak before they are ready may interfere with the mental processes involved in *restructuring* (or re-organizing) their internal mental grammar. For this reason, many of the activities you will find in the *Consolidation* stage are not speaking activities but simply *understanding* tasks. For example, students may be asked to read (or listen to) a series of sentences – some including structure X and some including structure Y – and to match these sentences with the appropriate pictures. These kinds of activities are sometimes called *grammar interpretation tasks,* because they require the learners to interpret the grammar item rather than simply produce it. Such activities involve what researchers call *input processing* (as opposed to *output processing*).

Finally, the third "P" in the equation we have called *Use*, but it is important to emphasize that the kind of use we are talking about it is *personalised use.* That is, learners are required to put the new item to work in ways that are relevant to them and their world. This is consistent with the view (outlined above) that language is only memorable when it has been "owned", that is, when it has been appropriated and put to use for the learner's own particular purposes. Asking learners to *personalise* new language is, of course, not without its risks. In order to mitigate these risks, it is important to observe the following principles:

1 be prepared to set an example yourself – that is, don't ask learners to do things that you wouldn't do, or won't do
2 allow the learners the relative privacy of pair and/or group work before asking them to personalise to the whole class
3 allow learners the right to "pass" if there are things they don't want to talk about – there is still a lot of benefit to be gained from hearing *other* learners talking
4 don't correct the learners' language errors without first providing feedback on *what* they have said or written. Eg, "That must have been exciting! By the way, we say *I felt nervous,* not *I fell nervous".* And always correct with discretion and sensitivity.

THE STAGES OF THE CREATIVE GRAMMAR PRACTICE LESSONS

Most of the *Creative Practice* lessons follow the same sequence of stages: lead-in, presentation of the model text, reconstruction of the model text, text creation and text sharing. We do not mean to suggest that this sequence should never be varied. However, general adherence to this sequence has the following advantages: a gradual lead-in to a lesson opens up a field of awareness; the model text, if conspicuously presented, affords intensive input of the target structure(s); reconstruction of the model text provides ample opportunity for guided practice; the writing phase (text creation) gives students a highly motivating opportunity to express themselves creatively and – given the previous phases of the lesson – accurately; the sharing of texts which follows injects the stimulating spark of student-to-student communication.

Lead-in activities

These are for:

1 generally warming everyone up and getting them ready to work in a foreign language;
2 developing awareness of and interest in the topic you're going to work with;
3 bringing known words back to mind and teaching new ones.

A basic lead-in activity is brainstorming. A few of our lessons don't come with lead-ins of their own. For these, brainstorming is a good way to start. Or you can borrow a lead-in from another lesson.

Presentation of model text

A model text is a short text which not only shows the written form of the target structure, but also clarifies its meaning/use/function. Presentation of the text (not to be confused with presentation of a given target structure in a text) is the process of familiarising the students with the model text. This can be done in various ways. You can dictate the text or they can read it on OHP or on a handout. Often, however, presentation phases involve the students more actively in the construction of the model text, eg, you begin with a gapped version and elicit the missing words from them.

Reconstruction of model text

Reconstruction of a model text can be done in spoken or written form. It is the process of eliciting from the students as accurately as possible the text presented to them earlier. The rationale of this stage is this: by remembering the model text the students can experience a feeling of success and gain ability in using the structure(s) accurately. In using different lessons from *Teaching Grammar Creatively* you will encounter various ways of organising text reconstruction, such as use of gesture, pictures and written prompts.

Text creation

This is where your students create their own text within the framework of the model they have been working with. Naturally, your students will often want to know new vocabulary. Supply the words they ask for or make sure they have access to a bilingual dictionary. We have favoured writing for this phase as experience has shown that students find it far easier to be creative in writing. Writing also allows greater focus on accuracy since students have the time to reflect, correct, discard and add. It allows text creation in pairs or small groups and can therefore generate much task-focused speaking. Finally, the products can be displayed and/or used in other ways.

If, however, you want your students to create their texts orally, we suggest the following procedure:

1 Form pairs or small groups.
2 Provide each group or pair with a cassette recorder.
3 Ask them to create a text orally. One of them says the text out loud and this text is recorded.
4 The students listen to the recording of the text. If they spot any errors, they make a new recording.
5 You listen to the cassette and comment on language correctness.
6 Students make a new recording incorporating your suggestions.
7 All the pairs or groups present their recordings to the class.

All this would hardly be possible in normal, unrecorded oral production.

BASIC TECHNIQUES

We have found the following techniques helpful in transferring the grammar structures (in the form of sentence fragments) into students' long term memory.

Silent time

H A Klauser (1986, p. 90) suggests allowing a period of silence before any creative writing. She claims that this 'daydreaming' or 'drifting off' is of great importance for getting ready to write. We are not suggesting here that a silent time before the creative writing is an absolute must, however, our students have always commented favourably on such a phase. It seems that the silent time helps them get into contact with their 'poetic selves' and thus access their creativity. (We sometimes use meditative music to accompany the silent time.)

Reading out loud by the teacher

In several lessons we suggest that you read out the model text after the learners have reconstructed it. Preferably, they should have their eyes closed. This 'straight-through' clear hearing of the text helps students to create a holistic image of it. The reading also provides a model of pronunciation and intonation; one that seems especially effective if students are reflectively listening with eyes closed. Finally, this reading can be essential as a means of 'anchoring' the structure and elements of the text in the minds of those students whose main channel of intake is auditory.

Managing students' reading out loud

Our experience is that students profit greatly from reading out loud themselves if and only if they have adequate rehearsal. The best known form of rehearsal is in teacher–led, whole class repetition of difficult words or phrases. But, if you are asking students to read out their own texts, more student-centred rehearsal is appropriate. Before asking students to read out loud, tell them to:

1 Read through their texts silently looking for words they aren't sure how to pronounce. They can then ask or check in a dictionary.
2 Rehearse by reading the text sub-vocally, that is by silently moving lips, tongue and other vocal 'apparatus'.
3 Practise making pauses so the audience can follow them well and using the pauses to make eye contact with their audience. Ask them to read out loud, clearly and slowly. Remind them that the audience suffers if a speaker's subconscious attitude while reading out loud is 'I want to get this over with as quickly as possible'.

Correction as editing

Errors are unavoidable when learners write texts. You need to understand this and treat learners' texts sympathetically. However, we have noticed that learners typically have a strong desire to improve the accuracy of their texts if they know that these will be shared later on (see 'Publication of the learners' texts' below). This follow-on accuracy work, or *editing,* is the process whereby the students *themselves,* other students, and/or you read their written work and suggest changes which can be incorporated in a new version of that work.

Editing takes place either while students are writing (you walk round and suggest changes) or after the students have finished. Editing is important since it increases learner awareness of appropriate forms. Also, for our method, learner texts need to be accurate since they serve as additional input in various follow-on activities (see 'Publication of learners' texts' and 'Anchoring' below).

It is important to let your students know that their texts will not be corrected as if they were tests. Your students should come to regard any correction as a means whereby they can better edit their work before sharing or 'publication'. Your attitude is decisive here: rather than tally errors, do everything necessary to help the learners with the process of finalising and improving their products. You can best do this by never using discouraging language. Klauser (1986, p. 89) recommends language such as 'I think you need ...', 'Maybe you could note ...', etc. The main options in the editing of student texts are:

1 The teacher as editor
   After finishing their texts, students hand them in and you correct all the errors. This can be done in class – while other students are still writing – or after the lesson.
2 The teacher as a gentle editor
   You correct only what you think your students cannot correct themselves. Underline auto-correctable errors (those you assume the students are able to correct themselves) in pencil. The students then go through their texts a second time trying to correct what you have underlined, possibly also consulting classmates, using a dictionary and/or checking with the model text(s). In an informal study we carried out with teenagers in their fourth year of English sixty percent of all the errors were successfully corrected using this editing mode.
3 Other learners as editors
   When students have finished writing, ask them to work in pairs and to exchange their texts. Get them to help each other by suggesting changes in the texts before these are handed in to you.

Publication of the learners' texts

We have found each of the following methods successful:

1 Regularly use a text-board to display (neat) copies of student texts, preferably together with other visuals selected by you and your students. Your text-board can be a cork-board set aside for this purpose or poster paper stuck on the walls of the classroom.

2 Get students to read out their texts to the class. Involve them in giving feedback, for example saying what they like about others' texts. This can contribute greatly to a readiness on the students' part to listen to each other and treat each other with respect.

3 Suggest that students collect their texts in a special individual or class journal. Getting your students to read their journal(s) from time to time can contribute enormously to their own assessment of their progress over a period of time.

Anchoring

The following techniques for helping students remember grammar points have proved helpful in our trial classes. You can teach some of them to your students so that they can use them on their own at home (or in class). Others are mainly for classroom use. After trying out some of these techniques, you might like to discuss their usefulness with your students in order to find out what works best.

Learners anchor their own texts

After the final editing, ask your students to memorise their own texts. This can be done in various ways:

1 By reading the first line of the text out loud. Once able to remember it, students add the second line and so on.

2 Students read the full text as often as necessary in order to be able to recite it completely. This may be accompanied by inner voicing or muttering, a technique especially effective for learners who are very auditory in their learning style.

3 Students read through the text. They try, while doing so, to form a striking mental image for each line, one that will help them to remember the line. Mental images can be visual representations of what has been read, or sounds, feelings, smells, or tastes or any combination of these. Closing the eyes can facilitate this mental imagery. (For example, see 1.7.)

4 Students can walk up and down saying the text to themselves line by line.

5 Students can write the text or parts of the text (especially the ones which are difficult to remember) in the air. They close their eyes and imagine seeing the text in the air or on an imaginary board or TV screen.

6 Students can record the text on a cassette recorder and learn it by listening to it several times.

7 Students can underline various parts of the text in different colours, draw on it or scribble down anything that will help them recall the text. If you are leading this work, give students some time to study the text. Then you/they remove it and they write it down from memory (in class or at home). Give them time to check their version with the original.

8 Work in pairs. Each learner produces a gapped version of their own text. Their partner should fill in the appropriate words in each gap. Depending on the level of the class, the words that have been omitted can be given in a box underneath the text. Alternatively, only the first letter of each missing word can be given.

9 Get students to work in pairs, each student dictating their own text to their partner. Each learner then corrects their partner's text.

Learners anchor someone else's text

After the final editing, display all the texts that your learners have written on the walls of the classroom. Ask everyone to stand up and choose one text that they would like to memorise (not their own).

Get them to copy this text into their own note book – without taking it off the wall. Students try to remember as much of these texts as they can, then go back to their desks and note down what they can remember. Then they go back to the texts again and so on.

Encourage your students to memorise the texts they have copied. Then collect all the texts from the wall and either ask for recitations of individual texts ('Who can quote Jose's text?') or read out some words from a text. See if anyone can recite the whole text or follow on from the bit you started with.

Learners anchor other texts

After the final editing, ask your learners to memorise as many texts as they can within a given time (eg, five minutes). Then arrange students in groups and get them to find out who can remember the most texts within each group.

Learners anchor parts of texts

1 Underline various parts of each text with different coloured pencils and display the texts on the walls of the classroom. (For example, underline individual words that you would like your class to remember in green, certain structures in red, other structures in blue.) Ask your learners to walk round and remember the underlined parts of the texts. Then call out one of the colours. The learners quote as many of the words and structures they can remember that were underlined in that colour.
2 Use a tambourine to beat the rhythm of one of the underlined sentences. The learners guess the sentence. (Thanks to Glen Stephen for this idea.)
3 Another technique involves all students reading several texts each and remembering sentences from them which they especially like. Give students time to memorise a set of favourite sentences in different texts. Ask them to quote the sentences they like without looking at the texts. This technique is especially effective in revision following a sequence of grammar exercises. (This technique is based on a model developed by Stevick.)

The CD-ROM

The CD-ROM accompanying this book contains two parts – an audio part and a CD-ROM part. The CD-ROM contains the following items:
· Text files of the model texts for all the lessons. This makes it easy for you to change the model texts so that they are more appropriate for the level of your students. You can edit the texts and print them out, or transfer them onto OHTs (or even put them into a PowerPoint presentation).
· Text files of worksheets and language boxes.
· Files containing all the artwork from the book. Again, you can print the drawings out or transfer them directly from your computer onto OHTs.
· Audio files of the model texts, for use in addition to or instead of your own reading out of the model texts. They can be played directly from your computer or from a CD player.

The following icons in the book will help you with selecting files:

 Text file / artwork on CD-ROM

Sound track on the audio part of the CD (playable on an audio CD player).

Each audio icon is numbered, so it will be easy to find the correct track.

CHAPTER 1
BASIC PHRASE PATTERNS

1.1 LANGUAGE OF DESCRIPTION

LEVEL
Lower intermediate +

TIME
40–60 minutes

Section A

AIMS:
– to introduce language of description
– to highlight the form and position of adjectives.

DISCOVERY

1. Write the following sentences on the board or project them using an OHP.

   a. *The bag has longs handles and bigs pockets.*
   b. *I have a suitcase very old.*
   c. *She was carrying a big and black umbrella.*
   d. *I bought a leather new jacket.*
   e. *It was a too expensive coat, so I didn't buy it.*
   f. *He was wearing a three-pieces suit.*
   g. *This sweater feels softly and looks nicely.*
   h. *What is a smallest size you have?*

2. Ask the students to correct the sentences, working first individually, and then in pairs or groups of three. Ask them to identify the rule that has been broken, in each case. (Alternatively, one student works on sentences a–d, while his or her partner works on sentences e–h. They then explain their corrections to each other).

3. Check the answers, and elicit the rule of adjective use that each sentence exemplifies, ie,

   a. *The bag has long handles and big pockets.* (= adjectives do not take plural forms)
   b. *I have a very old suitcase.* (= adjectives usually go in front of the noun)
   c. *She was carrying a big black umbrella.* (= two adjectives that are in front of the noun do not usually need to be joined with *and*)
   d. *I bought a new leather jacket.* (= words that say what something is made of, like *leather*, or what it is used for, go nearer to the noun than words that describe the colour, size, or age of the thing, like *new*).
   e. *The coat was too expensive, so I didn't buy it.* ('*too* + adjective' phrases do not usually go before the noun.)
   f. *He was wearing a three-piece suit.* (Adjectives made up of 'number + noun' do not have a plural form, even when the number is plural.)
   g. *This sweater feels soft and looks nice.* (Verbs like *feel, look, smell,* etc, take adjectives not adverbs.)
   h. *What is the smallest size you have?* (Superlative forms of adjectives usually take *the.*)

CONSOLIDATION

1. Read aloud a description of an object, such as the one below (you may want to adjust it to the level of the class), and ask the students to draw the object as you read. You may need to read it two or three times. They can then compare their drawings.

I've lost a valuable set of keys. There are five keys all in all, attached to a big plastic key ring. The key ring is heart-shaped and has the letters JR in the middle. The biggest key is long and rusty, and has just one big tooth. It is the key to my gate. I never use it, because the gate is always unlocked. The second key is tiny, and has a square plastic handle and lots of little teeth. It is the key to my post box. The third key is very thick and heavy and has two square-shaped teeth. That is my house key. I badly need it! The fourth key is the key to my office. It is a traditional, medium-sized Yale key with a circular handle and a row of wavy teeth. Finally, the last key is different from all the others: it is short and fat and has a sort of round mouth at one end with six little teeth that point out. What's that key for? Now, that's a secret!

2. As a follow up, ask individuals to describe their drawings while you draw their description on the board. Different students can take turns to describe different parts of the drawing. You can then read the original description and see if it matches.

USE

1. Ask the students to work in pairs. They take turns to describe something – such as an item of clothing, a piece of jewellery, a document, or even an animal! – that they once lost and never found. Their partner attempts to draw the thing, in the form of a LOST (or MISSING) notice. Together they can decide on an appropriate reward for finding the item, and write this under the drawing.

2. The notices can then be displayed around the class. Students can move from one to another, asking questions such as *Who lost the X? Where did you lose it? How much was it worth? What colour was it?* etc.

LEVEL
Lower intermediate +

TIME
40–60 minutes

EXTRAS
(Optional) class set of handouts of yes/no questions; class set of handouts of skeleton text

Section B

LEAD-IN ACTIVITIES

• Guessing objects

1. Ask everyone in class to think of an object.
2. After a while, choose a student and start asking yes/no questions in order to find out what object they have in mind. For example:

Is it in this room?
Is it made of ... ?
Is it expensive / cheap / red / ... ?
Is it longer / smaller than a ... ?
Is it as big / expensive / ... as ...?
Can you ... ?
Have you got one?
Do you need it every day?

Repeat with several students so that your class get an opportunity to hear a range of questions several times. To give your students further practice in asking questions, pair them up and let them repeat this guessing game over the course of a few lessons.

Variation

1. Ask your students to split up into three or four groups and to sit or stand in different corners of the room.
2. Ask one member of each group to come to you. Show them a word for an object, e.g. *umbrella.*
3. The 'messengers' go back to their groups. The members of each group have to ask their messenger questions to find out what the object is. The messengers are, of course, not allowed to give any help by mime or gesture, etc. When a group has guessed the object they send another messenger to you to be shown the next word. The group that guesses three words in a row first wins.

• An object that means something to me

1. Talk briefly about an object that means something to you. For example:

I've had this bag for years. I got it from a friend who bought it in India and gave it to me as a present. Its colours are not bright any more but I still like it. It smells nice and I sometimes think of India when I look at it.

2. Ask the students to close their eyes and visualise an object that is special to them. Allow two or three minutes for this.
3. Tell them to get into groups of three and to talk about their object.

• **Listen and guess**

1. Read out text A twice. (Don't fill in the blank.) Before the second reading, ask your students to close their eyes and imagine the object as vividly as possible.

Text A
Too many people write about love.
I want to write about my _____
It's brown and smooth,
a present from Dad.
I've had it since I was nine
and I've always found it again
when I've lost it.
I sometimes smell it
when I put it on
and it always reminds me
of saddles and horses.

2. Ask your students to say what they think the object is. (It's a belt.)

PRESENTATION OF MODEL TEXTS

1. Present texts B and C on the board or provide photocopies.
2. Ask the students to fill in the blanks for both texts.

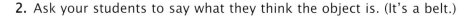

Text B
Too m _____ p _____ w _____ about l _____ .
I w _____ to write about my t _____ b _____
I don't r _____ when I g _____ it.
But it has been s _____ on
my b_____
f _____ a l _____ t _____ .
It l _____ o _____ and worn
but I would n _____ t _____ it away.
I l _____ it.

Text C
T _____ many p _____ write about love.
I w _____ to write about my e _____ r _____ .
They are g _____ with r _____ f _____
and I do not r _____ how
long I have h _____ them.
They l _____ f _____
and when I s _____ m _____ in the mirror
I s _____.

3. Read out the original texts (see keys on next page). Get your students to listen and check what they have filled in.

Text B (key)
Too many people write about love.
I want to write about my teddy bear.
I don't remember when I got it.
But it has been sitting on
my bookshelf
for a long time.
It looks old and worn
but I would never throw it away.
I love it.

Text C (key)
Too many people write about love
I want to write about my earrings.
They are green with red flowers
and I do not remember how
long I have had them
They look funny
and when I see myself in the mirror
I smile.

TEXT CREATION

1. Write the following prompts on the board. Ask your students to write their own text based on these prompts.

Too many people write about love.
I want to _____
I _____ (since / for _____)
_____
It's _____

2. After editing (see p. 10) get some students to read out their texts to the class.

Here are two texts, the one on the left written by a thirteen-year-old, the one on the right by Janice Tabe at a teacher training workshop.

Too many people write about love.
I want to write about my skateboard.
It's a present from my parents and I like it very much.
It was very expensive and the deck alone cost a fortune.
It's black and green and looks fantastic
It's the best present I've ever had.

Too many people write about love.
I want to write about my big feet.
I don't remember when I got them but they've been at the end of my legs for a long time.
They look old and worn but I would never cut them off.
I need them.

1.2 SOMETHING IS THE COLOUR OF ...

LEVEL
Lower intermediate +

TIME
40–60 minutes

Section A

AIM:
– to show how verbs of the senses are complemented, either with nouns or adjectives

DISCOVERY

1. Draw the following table on the board, and ask students to copy it:

Your brother	looks	like	David Beckham.

(You can change the name of the person in the last column, of course!)

2. Dictate these words and ask the students to write the words in the correct column in the table:

sounds
that music
techno
she
Britney Spears
smells
this soap
lemon
tastes
this stuff
peanut butter
feels
leather

3. Check the task, by, for example, asking individual students to come to the board and fill in the columns.

4. Draw a second table on the board, like this, which the students should copy:

Your brother	looks	cute.

5. Repeat the activity by dictating these words:

cool
that music
sounds
she
smart
this soap
good
smells
tastes
this stuff
horrible
feels
your skin
smooth

6. Again, check the task. Students can also check in pairs.

7. Now, ask learners to study the two tables, and explain the difference between them. The key is in the last column: in the first table, the words in the last column are all nouns, while in the second table they are all adjectives. The rule is: 'sense verb + *like* + noun', or 'sense verb + adjective'.

CONSOLIDATION

1. Write the following table on to the board, or onto an overhead transparency:

Yuk! That cheese smells	smooth and soft.
Yummy! This ice-cream tastes	like roses.
Mmmm. Your skin feels so	like wool.
Interesting. This artificial meat tastes	disgusting.
Mmm. Your perfume smells	depressed.
Someone's at the door. It sounds	like rain.
What's your jacket made of? It feels	delicious.
What's the matter? You look	like the neighbour's dog.
What's that barking? It sounds	like chicken.
Take an umbrella. It looks	like the postman.

(You can change the vocabulary in this table to match the level of the learners.)

2. Ask learners, working in pairs, to match the sentence halves in each column. Point out that there is often more than one way of matching the two halves of the sentences, but there is one answer that is *more likely* than the others.

3. Now, ask learners to choose some *unlikely* (but grammatically correct) matchings. For example, *Yummy! This ice-cream tastes like chicken.* They should then invent a context for this sentence, eg, *The fox and the wolf were on holiday. They stopped to buy some ice-cream. Yummy, said the fox, this ice-cream tastes like chicken!*

4. Ask students read out their contexts to the rest of the class. They can vote on the best "crazy context".

USE

1. Ask students to each draw a five pointed star on a piece of paper. On the first point of the star they should write a word that evokes a memorable experience involving *sight* – for example, a spectacular sunset, or a firework display. On the second point of the star they should write a word that evokes a memory involving *hearing;* on the third, a word associated with a memory of *touch;* on the fourth, *smell* and on the fifth, *taste.*

2. The students then form pairs or groups of three. They show one another their "memory stars" and ask and answer questions about the experiences that each point of the star represents. For example, *What does this mean? What happened to you? Where were you? How did you feel? What did it look/feel/taste/etc like?* You can write these questions on the board, and slowly erase them (or parts of them) as students become used to using them.

3. Individuals from each group can report to the class something interesting they heard in their conversation.

LEVEL
Lower intermediate +

TIME
50 minutes

EXTRAS
(Optional) OHP transparency with model text

Section B

LEAD-IN ACTIVITIES

• Story telling

1. Write the following words on the board. Explain any your students are not familiar with:
   love   hatred   fear   boredom   anger
   disappointment   happiness   sadness   joy

2. Talk about two or three incidents from your life exemplifying the emotions above, for example:
   I once spent a night alone on a lonely beach. When it was dark, I could suddenly hear all kinds of unfamiliar sounds and noises. I began to be afraid there might be snakes, spiders and scorpions. And then I was seized with the fear that somebody might come along and kill me. I finally fell asleep but I had bad dreams.
   Another incident I remember is once coming upon a group of boys who were holding an animal down. When they noticed me they let go of it and I saw that they had tied a big plastic toy to a cat's tail. The cat ran off miaowing. I ran after it, caught it, and, after a struggle, managed to cut the string with my pocket knife. I was very angry with those boys, but they ran away while I was trying to help the animal.

3. Ask your students to work in groups of three or four. Tell them to pick one word from the box and to make notes about an incident or situation that goes with their word.

4. In their groups they then take turns reading out their notes. (They don't need to make sentences.) The other group members try to guess what emotion the incident/situation was all about. The author confirms or denies the guesses and elaborates as requested.

PRESENTATION OF MODEL TEXT

Show your students the gapped text on the OHP (or write it on the board) and ask them to guess the missing words. Whenever someone has guessed a word correctly, fill it in.

Gapped text
Happiness _____ the colour of poppies in spring.
It _____ like chocolate ice cream.
It _____ like peach blossom.
It _____ like the cry of the eagle
and it _____ like the wide open sky.

Model text
Happiness is the colour of poppies in spring.
It tastes like chocolate ice cream.
It smells like peach blossom.
It sounds like the cry of the eagle
and it looks like the wide open sky.

Track 02

TEXT CREATION

1. Write a list of feelings on the board. Ask your students to choose one feeling from the list. Everyone writes their own text based on the structure of the model text. If you want to give your students some more examples before they start writing, there are three texts below which were written by thirteen–year–old learners in their third year of English.

2. When finished, students read their texts out loud or display them in the classroom.

Example texts

Happiness is the colour of red flowers.
It smells like the flowers in a small garden.
Happiness sounds like the singing of a hippo in the water.
Happiness makes me dance rock and roll.

Hatred is the colour of black and red devils.
It tastes like a bitter lemon,
it smells like death
and it looks like the darkest night.
Hatred sounds like thunder.
It makes me feel depressed.

Fear is the colour of a grey, polluted river.
It smells like the fumes of factories
and it looks like a ghost.
It sounds like the howling of wolves.
Fear makes me think of problems.

1.3 *THERE IS ...*

Section A

AIM:
– to teach or review the use of *there is/there are* for description

DISCOVERY

1. Display the following cartoon and ask the students to fill in the missing line.

Alternatively, supply the following sentences and ask the students to choose the best one:

> *A fly is in my soup.*
> *My soup has a fly in it.*
> *There's a fly in my soup.*
> *In my soup is a fly.*

2. Elicit other customer complaints for these waiter responses:

> *Yes, sir, it's cockroach soup.*
> *Yes, sir, it's hair soup.*
> *Yes, sir, it's tomato soup.*
> *Yes, sir, it's chicken soup.*
> *Yes, sir, it's elephant soup.*
> *Yes, sir, it's two–flies soup.*

3. Write the sentences on the board, and draw attention to the use of *There is/are ...* to announce the presence of something.

CONSOLIDATION

1. Display the picture on page 27 using an overhead projector, or by making and distributing photocopies. If using photocopies, make sure that these are distributed face-down, and that the students do not look at them until given a signal.

Note: If it is not possible to reproduce this picture, any large poster or wallchart will do, so long as it includes a number of features, and does not present a problem in terms of too much unfamiliar vocabulary.

2. Allow the class half a minute to study the picture, then mask it (or ask students to turn their copies over). Dictate the following sentences: students write them down while at the same time they decide if they are true or false (Alternatively, simply read the sentences out, and the students tell you if they are true or false, without writing them down.) In the case of sentences that students judge to be false, elicit a correction.

There is a lion.
There is a man with two dogs.
There is one duck walking and there are two ducks flying.
There is a woman sitting on a chair.
There are some butterflies.
There is a man carrying a basket.
There are three men carrying animals.
There is a man with a bow and arrow.

3. Check the task by revealing the picture again.

USE

1. Organise the class into pairs. Ask students to visualise a view that they are familiar with and that has particular associations, eg, the view from their bedroom window, or a place where they once spent a holiday. In pairs they take turns to describe the view to their partner, who can ask questions about it. (As an alternative, the partner can attempt to draw the scene.) To help them, you could, beforehand, describe a view of your own, using expressions like *near ..., farther away ..., in the distance ..., on the left/right ..., in the middle ...,* and write these on the board.

2. Each student then attempts to describe the scene *back* to the original student, who judges its accuracy, eg, *Yes, that's more or less how I described it*, or *You forgot the ....*

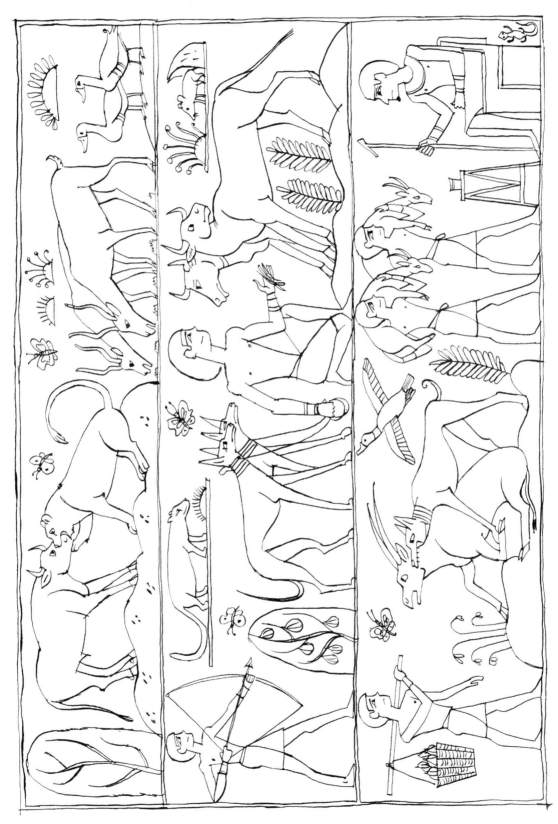

LEVEL
Elementary +

TIME
50 minutes

EXTRAS
(Optional) class set of handouts of worksheets A and B; ten paper strips (40 x 15 cm each); Blu-Tack

Section B

PREPARATION
For Step 2 of the variation on p. 30, make strips of paper with words/word groups on them.

LEAD-IN ACTIVITIES
• **Make your choice**
1. Hand out photocopies of worksheet A below. If photocopying is not possible, write the texts and the missing words on the board or on an OHP.
2. Tell the students to fill in the blanks with words from the box to create two meaningful texts. Make sure everyone understands the last two lines of each text.

WORKSHEET A

There are_____   *There are _____*
there are _____   *there are _____*
there are _____   *there are _____*
there are _____   *there are _____*
and _____   *and _____*
when I take a long look   *when I look out of my*
into your eyes.   *little tent in the dunes.*

> *kites of every colour – high mountains*
> *– flowers – tigers – white clouds –*
> *fireworks over dark lakes – tall trees*
> *– high waves – seagulls crying –*
> *surfboards jumping*

3. Get several students to read out their texts.
4. Ask your students which of the class's texts they like best.
5. Then read out the texts below.

WORKSHEET A (KEY)

There are flowers   *There are white clouds*
there are tigers   *there are seagulls crying*
there are tall trees   *there are high waves*
there are high mountains   *there are surfboards jumping*
and fireworks over dark lakes *and kites in all colours*
when I take a long look   *when I look out of my*
into your eyes.   *little tent in the dunes.*

TEXT CREATION
The students write their own texts using the gapped texts in worksheet A as models. They read out their texts or display them.

Variations

a. You may choose to offer only the following prompts:

There are _____

there are _____

there are _____

there are _____

and _____

when _____

b. You may offer them additional text endings, such as:

in the picture I'm going to paint

when I'm daydreaming in the classroom

when I'm looking down from my hang glider

when I remember ...

in the film I'd like to *make*

when I think of ...

PRESENTATION OF MORE MODEL TEXTS

1. Hand out copies of worksheet B or write the texts on the board and proceed in the same way as Steps 1–5 on p.28.

WORKSHEET B

There is _____   *There is* _____

there is _____   *there is* _____

there is _____   *there is* _____

there is _____   *and* _____

and _____   *in the town I hate living in.*

in the film I'd like to make.

> *a gangster – too little sun – no park*
> *– a sheriff – a carriage – a small*
> *town – lots of gold – a lot of traffic*
> *– too much* noise

2. When the students have read out their texts, present the key:

WORKSHEET B (KEY)

There is a small town   *There is a lot of traffic*

there is a sheriff   *there is too much noise*

there is a gangster   *there is too little sun*

there is a carriage   *and no park*

and lots of gold   *in the town I hate living in.*

in the film I'd like to make.

TEXT CREATION

1. Again, you have a choice of prompts. Depending on the level and creativity of your group, you can include the last sentence in the model. One student who was offered all the prompts, including the last sentence, wrote this:

There is a swimming pool
there is a cinema
there is a park
there is a nice school
and lots of sun
in the town I love living in.

2. Encourage everyone to write texts using both *there are* and *there is* in their texts. Get students to also include quantifiers *such as lots of, hardly any, few,* etc.

Variation

1. Write the following on the board:

There are _____	*There are* _____
there are _____	*there are* _____
there are _____	*there are* _____
and there are _____	*and there are* _____
in the classroom I like.	*when I look out of my*
	little tent on the beach.

2. Make strips of paper bearing these words:

white curtains	*beautiful kites*	*high waves*	*friendly teachers*

surfboards	*lots of posters*	*comfortable chairs*	*white clouds*

Stick the strips on the board. Ask some students to come to the board, take a strip and put it in the right gap.

3. Next, repeat steps 1 and 2 using the following prompts:

There is _____	*There is* _____
there is _____	*there is* _____
there is _____	*there is* _____
there is _____	*there is* _____
and _____	*in the town I do not like living in.*
in the film I'd like to make.	

and strips bearing the following:

much noise	*a sheriff*	*no park*	*a carriage*

a small town	*a gangster*	*no playground*	*a lot of traffic*	*lots of gold*

1.4 *SOMETHING ...*

LEVEL
Lower intermediate +

TIME
40–60 minutes

Section A

AIMS:
– to contrast the use of *something* and *anything*
– to highlight the different ways of complementing *something/anything*.

DISCOVERY

1. Hide a small object – such as a coin – in one hand, and put both hands behind your back. Tell the class: *I've got something in one hand. I haven't got anything in the other hand.* As soon as they say *Your left hand* or *Your right hand*, hold out that hand and show them that it is empty. When they nominate the other hand, bring out that hand, but don't open it. Tell them: *You have to guess what it is.* When they have guessed correctly, you can show them what you were hiding – or even give it to the student who guessed correctly!

2. Ask the class to recall what it was you said initially. Write these two sentences on the board, underlining the indefinite pronouns:

   I've got <u>something</u> in one hand.
   I haven't got <u>anything</u> in the other hand.

   Ask the students to explain the difference between the use of the two underlined words, ie, that *something* is used in positive contexts, while *anything* is (generally) used in negative contexts.

   Note: *Anything* is often used in questions, too, but *something* is possible if the person who is asking the question has already got an idea of what the *thing* is. Compare:

   Have you got anything to tell me?
   Have you got something to tell me?

CONSOLIDATION

1. Read out the following sentences, pausing briefly between them, and stopping after each pair of sentences to ask the class to guess what it is you are describing (but don't tell them if their guesses are correct until the end):

   It isn't anything you can eat;
   it's something you can admire.

   It isn't anything you can touch;
   it's something you can see.

   It isn't anything you can own;
   it's something that belongs to no one.

   It isn't anything that moves;
   it's something that always stays the same.

It isn't anything on this earth;
it's something out in space.

It isn't anything that you can see by day;
it's something you can only see at night.
(*Answer: a star*)

2. Ask the students if they can remember any of the sentences. Write the following prompts on the board to help them:

eat
admire

touch
see

own
belongs to

moves
the same

earth
space

by day
at night

USE

1. Write the following table on the board:

Is it something	(that) you ... (?)
It isn't anything	to ... (?) in/on/at ... (?)

2. Demonstrate the activity by telling the class that they have to guess a mystery object, ie, one that you are thinking of. The object should be something that you are wearing or that you have in your bag, briefcase, etc, and that has personal significance for you. To ask questions about it, students have to use phrases from the table. For example: *Is it something you can eat? Is it something to write with? Is it something in your bag?* Reply to each question using the formula *It isn't anything ...* When the class has guessed the item, show it to them, and encourage them to ask you questions about it, such as *How long have you had it? Who gave it to you? Why is it special?* (You can write some of these questions on the board.)

3. Organise the class into pairs or small groups, and each student takes a turn to think of a mystery object. The others try to guess what it is, and once they have done so, they should ask more general questions about it.

4. Ask individuals from different groups to report any interesting "discoveries".

LEVEL
Lower intermediate +

TIME
40 minutes

EXTRAS
Handouts of a model text; realia or pictures from home; a class set of blank slips of paper

Section B

PREPARATION

1. In the lesson before, ask students to bring a favourite present or a picture of it to the next class. You bring something too.
2. Make one photocopy of the model text for each group of four students. Cut each copy up into line by line strips.
3. Make a class set of blank slips of paper. The slips need only be big enough for students to write their names on.

LEAD-IN ACTIVITIES

• The teacher's favourite present

Show your present around and/or tell your class a story based upon it. In your story, say who you got it from, where and when you got it, and also why this is one of your favourite presents.

• The students' favourite presents

1. Divide the class into groups of four. One student in each group starts by showing their present, but doesn't talk about it at first. The other members of the group should speculate about the object and come up with a short background story about it. Ask them to include in their stories who their classmate got the present from, when and where they got it and why it is a favourite.
2. The student whose present it is then tells the real story behind it.

• Gift giving

1. Arrange your class in a big circle. Give everyone a pen and paper.
2. Give each student a strip of paper to write their name on.
3. Collect the strips, then hand them out again to different people.
4. Ask everyone to imagine that they are going to give a present to the student whose name they received. Give them time to think what they would give. Give a few examples (including symbolic gifts):

Monica, my present to you is a big meadow with lots of beautiful flowers and butterflies.
Michael, for you I have a magic ball. Whenever you touch it, you will hear a beautiful tune.
Tom, here is my present to you: a tiny little box. When you open it, you will find a picture in it. It is a special picture with a golden frame. The picture changes all the time and you always see in it what you want to see.

Stress that everyone must avoid judging or putting people down when giving a present. (For example, if anyone knows their partner has recently told a lie like having been unable to do homework because of a dentist appointment, they do not give *truth* as a present, instead they should choose something completely different, such as a computer that does a person's homework for them when they don't feel like doing it themselves.) If teaching teenagers, remind them to give the gift with humour and a sense of fun, not with sarcasm.

5. Everyone offers their gifts, one after the other.

PRESENTATION OF MODEL TEXT
1. Form groups. Give a cut-up copy of the model text to each group.
2. Ask the groups to arrange the lines so as to recreate the original.
3. When they have finished, get them to read out their texts to the class. Then read out the original for the students to check.

Model text
My birthday

*For my birthday
you can give me
something to play with
or something that I can use
or something very small
but please don't give me
anything my sister might like
and don't give me anything
that is purple or pink.*

TEXT RECONSTRUCTION
1. Ask each group to lay out the strips in the order shown above.
2. Ask them to study the text carefully.
3. Collect the strips.
4. Write the following prompts on the board. Help your learners to reconstruct the text orally. Give several learners a chance to say the whole text.

*For _____
_____ give me
something _____
or _____
or _____
but please don't _____
anything _____
and don't _____
_____ .*

TEXT CREATION
Ask students to write their own texts based on the model text. Display these texts in class, together with the visuals your students have brought along to class.
Here are two texts written by thirteen-year-old students:

*For my birthday
you can give me
some things I can use to play with
or something like a small book,*

but please don't give me
any toy cars or any dolls.

For my birthday
you can give me
a book or a game
but please don't give me an animal
or anything to eat
or anything that is very big,
because my room is very small.

Model text for adults

For my birthday
you can give me
something to read
or something to listen to
or you could take me out
to a restaurant,
but don't give me
another umbrella or purse
and, please, don't give me
anything to wear.
You know, I hate
taking things back.

1.5 *YOU'D BETTER* + BARE INFINITIVE

LEVEL
Lower intermediate +

TIME
40–60 minutes

Section A

AIMS:
– to review different ways of giving advice
– to introduce the use of *you'd better* + bare infinitive.

DISCOVERY

1. Draw a circle in the centre of the board and write the word *advice* in it; draw three or four lines radiating from the circle. Ask the students, working in pairs, to think of different ways, in English, of offering advice. Elicit advice expressions and write them on the board at the ends of the radiating lines. Expressions that may come up include *you should ...; you ought to ...* and *if I were you, I'd ....* Ask students to provide complete sentences using these structures for situations such as advising someone who has toothache, or a headache, or hiccoughs, or insomnia. Write example sentences on the board, such as *You should see a dentist.* (If *you'd better ...* is suggested at this stage, write it up and skip the next step.)

2. At the end of one line, write the word *better* and ask the students to think of an advice structure using this word. If none is forthcoming, add *see a dentist* after *better*. Pause, and then add *´d* in front of *better*. Finally, add *you*. If this is obviously new to the students, give them time to write it down, and ask different individuals to repeat the whole sentence. Point out that *´d* is a contraction of *had.*

CONSOLIDATION

1. Write the following sentence halves on the blackboard, or photocopy and distribute them. Ask the students to match the sentence halves so that all the matched halves make likely sentences.

You'd better wear a tie	if you want to lose weight.
You'd better make a reservation	if you want me to take you out.
You'd better join a gym	if you want to be sure of a seat.
You'd better be nice to me	if you want to pass the test.
You'd better take an umbrella	if you want to make a good impression.
You'd better do your homework	if you don't want to get wet.

2. They then work in pairs to write a short dialogue which incorporates one of the completed sentences. Different pairs can be assigned different sentences.

Alternatively, copy the table and cut it into its 12 sections, each section being one half of a sentence. Give one section to each student. They must memorise what is on their slip of paper and then walk around, repeating their half sentence, until they find the person whose half sentence matches theirs. Once they have found their "other half", they should then write a short dialogue which incorporates the complete sentence. (If there are more than 12 students in the class, make extra copies of the sentence halves so that there are enough to go round.)

USE

1. Ask students each to think of a situation or a person that is worrying or annoying them. You can give an example of your own, eg, a noisy neighbour, all the homework you have to mark this weekend, the overdue library books you haven't returned. Elicit some advice from the class, and prompt students to use *You'd better ...* as in *You'd better take them back!*

2. Ask students to stand in two parallel lines (A and B), facing each other. Students take turns to relate their problem while their partner opposite listens and then offers advice. Then the student at the top of line A moves to the bottom of the same line, and each student in that line moves up one space. Students re-tell their problems to their new partners, who offer advice. This continues until all the students in line A have interacted with all the students in line B. They then return to their seats. Ask individuals to report on the best advice they were given.

(If the class size or classroom layout doesn't allow this kind of formation, the students can first do the task with their immediate partner, and then be re-positioned so that they are able to interact with at least two other students successively.)

Note

Should and *ought to* are often used to talk generally – eg, *You should go to the dentist regularly. Had better* is used for specific, often urgent, cases: eg, *You'd better see your dentist about that tooth.*

LEVEL
Lower intermediate +

TIME
40 minutes

EXTRAS
None

Section B

LEAD-IN ACTIVITIES

1. Write *You'd better ...* on the board and ask your students to finish the sentence orally. Elicit clarification of the situation given in each sentence by asking everybody *who* said their sentence and *to whom*. For example:

    Student: You'd better give up smoking.
    Teacher: Who said that?
    Student: A girl?
    Teacher: And who to?
    Student: To her boyfriend.

2. Tell your class to get into groups of four. The students' task is to each write at least three sentences in three to five minutes. Each learner in turn then reads out a sentence and the others guess the situation.
3. The groups decide which of the situations are the commonest.
4. The groups report their findings to the whole class.

PRESENTATION AND RECONSTRUCTION OF MODEL TEXT

1. Present the gapped text on the board.

'You'd better w _____ h _____
you'd better p _____ m _____
a _____ at s _____
you'd better t _____ up your r _____
you'd better p _____ on a w _____ s _____;
they s _____
I u _____, b _____ I d _____ c _____
and I d _____ even k _____ why not.

2. The students try to guess the missing words. Help through mime, gesture and hints like opposites, synonyms, grammatical categories, etc. Whenever a student calls out a correct word, fill it in.
3. Read the full model text out.

Model text
'You'd better work harder
you'd better pay more
attention at school
you'd better tidy up your room
you'd better put on a warm sweater,'
they say.
I understand, but I don't care
and I don't even know why not.

4. Ask your learners to study the gapped text for a minute or so. Then remove it/rub it out and ask several students to recite the full text from memory.

TEXT CREATION

1. The students write their own texts using the following skeleton. (You can, of course, change it depending on the level and age of your group.)

'You'd better _____
you'd better _____
you'd better _____,
you'd better _____,'
_____ say.
_____ understand, but _____ care
and _____ even know why not.

2. Ask some of your students to read out their texts. The rest of the class tries to guess the situation behind each text.

Variation

If you work with adults you may want to use the following model text.

'You'd better try harder,'
that's what my boss said.
'You'd better be on time,'
that's what my boss said.
'You'd better use your head,'
that's what my boss said.
'You'd better be friendlier,'
that's what I thought.
'I'd better be leaving,'
that's what I said.

TEXT RECONSTRUCTION

1. Split your class into two groups.
2. Read out the model text in a rhythmic way.
3. Invite everybody to chant with you.
4. Get group one to chant line one, group two to chant line two. Proceed like this with the rest of the text.

1.6 *HOW LONG DID IT TAKE YOU ...?*

LEVEL
Lower intermediate +

TIME
40–60 minutes

Section A

AIMS:
– to introduce the phrase *it takes X* + time expression + *to*-infinitive
– to practise asking and answering questions about duration.

DISCOVERY
1. Say the sentence *It took me an hour to find a taxi* in the students' own language and ask them to tell you how to say this in English. If the students don't know, write the English equivalent on the board.

If the class is multi-lingual, present the following situation:

"I needed a taxi. I started looking for one. An HOUR later I finally found one. How can you summarise that in English, in a sentence beginning *It ...?*"

2. Ask students to supply other words or phrases that could substitute for *an hour* (eg, *thirty minutes*), *to find a taxi* (eg, *to get home*), and *me* (eg, *her*). Elicit the present tense of *took*. Write all these alternatives on the board so as to form a table:

It took	me	an hour	to find a taxi
It takes	her	thirty minutes	to get home

3. Elicit the questions for each of the above sentences, ie, *How long did it take you to find a taxi? How long does it take her to get home?* and write these up as well.

CONSOLIDATION
1. Write the following sentences on the board, or project them using an overhead projector. Then dictate the following numbers: *ten, twenty, eight, thirty, two, one, six,* and *eighty*. Ask the students, working in pairs or small groups, to decide which number goes in which sentence.

1. *It takes sunlight ... minutes to reach the Earth.*
2. *It took Columbus ... months to cross the Atlantic Ocean.*
3. *It would take a spaceship ... months to reach Mars.*
4. *It took the Greeks ... years to conquer Troy.*
5. *It takes the moon ... days to go round the Earth.*
6. *It took Phileas Fogg ... days to go round the world.*
7. *It took the Ancient Egyptians ... years to build the Great Pyramid.*
8. *It took me ... hour to plan this lesson.*

[Answers:
1. eight
2. two
3. six
4. ten
5. thirty
6. eighty
7. twenty
8. one – of course, you can change this to suit yourself!]

2. Check the answers – students can amend their own – and then ask them to turn their papers over. Ask a student the question *How long did it take the Greeks to conquer Troy?* (Answer: *Ten years.*) In pairs or small groups, the students do the same, asking questions to test each other's memories of the facts.

USE

Organise the class into groups of three or four. Tell them that they are going to conduct a survey to see who is the class "slowcoach" (ie, the slowest person in the class), and the class "speedy Gonzalez", ie, the fastest person in the class. In groups, they should prepare five – six questions, such as *How long does it take you to get dressed in the morning?* They then circulate, asking and answering their questions and noting down the answers. They return to their original groups to collate their answers. Finally, they report their findings to the class, and their verdict on who is the slowest/fastest to do things. (Note: to defuse any negative judgements about "being slow", you can remind the class of two English sayings: *Slow and steady wins the race*; and *More haste, less speed!)*

LEVEL
Lower intermediate +

TIME
50 minutes

EXTRAS
A class set of the map

Section B

PREPARATION
Make a class set of the map below.

LEAD-IN ACTIVITIES
• **How long did it take them?**
1. Distribute the maps (see figure 1 below)

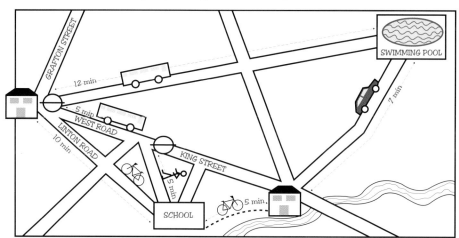

2. Write 'How long did it take Sue, Tony and Sandra to get to the swimming pool after school?' on the board. Read out the following text twice.

Sue rode her bike along the river to her house. Then five minutes later, her mother took her to the swimming pool by car. Tony rode his bike to his house at the corner of Grafton Street and Linton Road and then waited 3 minutes for the bus, which he took to the swimming pool. Sandra walked to the bus stop in King Street and took the bus to the swimming pool.

3. Ask your students how long it took the three pupils to get to the pool. Read the text again if no one knows.

• **Reporting**
1. Write the following on the board.
It took me _____ hours / days / weeks / months / quite a long time / years to _____
It took me only _____

2. Tell your students about something that took you quite a long time to learn, such as:
You know, when I was about six or seven I had problems figuring out which was 'right' and which was 'left'. It took me quite a long time to be able to say which was which. What helped me in the end was that I had a scar on my right hand for quite a time and so I remembered where 'right' was.

3. Then tell them about something that took you only a short time to do or learn or find out about, such as:

When I started studying at college, I realised that it was very important to be able to type. So I went to this three week course. But after a week, I knew I had already learned what I wanted to learn. So it really took me only a week to learn to type.

4. Ask your students to think of situations in which they experienced something that took quite a time and something that worked surprisingly fast. Tell them to write down not more than seven key words.

5. Get your class to work in groups of three or four.

6. Group members take turns reading out their key words. The others try to guess the situation, for example:
Student 1: smoker / give up / start again / three years
Student 2: You smoked a lot and tried to give it up, but you always started again. That was three years ago.
Student 1: No, it took me three years to stop; I don't smoke any more.

7. Each member of the class reports about another member of their group, using the following prompt (write it on the board if necessary):

I found it interesting that it (only) took
_____ (only) _____ to _____

Example:
I found it interesting that it (only) took Aiyumi (only) two years to learn as much English as she can speak now.

PRESENTATION OF MODEL TEXT
1. Write the first letters of each word of the model text on the board. Students guess the text. Help, if necessary, by adding more letters, giving synonyms and opposites, or by using mime or gesture.

Model text
It took him an hour
to answer my question
and it took him two days to say,
'I can't come to your party'
and a week to ring me back.
It took him six months
to write me a letter
and it will take him years
to find out
what he wants.
Phew, isn't he slow?

2. Then read the text out loud to give your students a pronunciation model. Ask them to repeat the text out loud.

Alternatively you may hand out a copy of the model text. Ask your students to read through the text and to form mental images for each of the situations described in the text in order to facilitate memorising the model text. Then ask them to repeat the text out loud to themselves.

TEXT CREATION

1. Write the following on the board and ask the learners to write their own texts.

It took him/her/them _____ (only)

_____

Phew, isn't/aren't he/she/they slow (fast).

2. The students can then present their texts to the class. Here are two examples:

It took him a year to learn to read,
and it took him eight months
to understand how to work with a
computer.
It also took him some weeks
to finish the biology project.
It takes him days
to learn a text by heart.
But it takes him only a minute
to stir up a fight in our class.

It took my girlfriend only half an hour
to learn to ice-skate and
it took her only five minutes
to learn a long text by heart.
It also took her only four days
to read a book a thousand pages
long
and it took her only two days
to learn for a difficult test.
Phew, isn't she fast!

1.7 USED TO

LEVEL
Lower intermediate +

TIME
40–60 minutes

Section A

AIMS:
– to introduce/review *used to* to speak about past habits
– to contrast *used to* with ways of expressing present habits, such as *usually*.

DISCOVERY

1. Prepare five sentences about yourself, describing your habits and routines, some of which are true and some false, and at least two of which incorporate the structure *used to*. For example:

   I generally do all my shopping on Saturdays.
   I usually spend Sunday with the family.
   I used to go rock climbing a lot.
   I don't often go to the cinema.
   I never used to like cooking, but now I do.

2. Dictate the sentences to the students, and check that they are familiar with the vocabulary. Allow them to compare their sentences with a partner. Elicit back the sentences, each one from a different student, and write them on the board. Alternatively ask individuals to come up and write a sentence each on the board.

3. Tell the class that some of the sentences are true and some false, and ask them to guess which. Allow them time to discuss this, before soliciting ideas. Challenge them to give reasons for their choices. Finally, tell them the answers.

4. Draw attention to the sentences and ask the students, working in pairs, to divide them into two groups according to *grammatical* criteria. Elicit suggestions and acknowledge their acceptability, where appropriate. Some students, for example, might divide the above sentences into affirmative vs negative. If no group has chosen *past vs present habits* as the criterion, tell the class that you have divided them into the following two groups, and challenge them to work out the difference:

   Group A:
   I generally do all my shopping on Saturdays.
   I usually spend Sunday with the family.
   I don't often go to the cinema.

   Group B:
   I used to go rock climbing a lot.
   I never used to like cooking, but now I do.

   If necessary, underline the instances of *used to* in Group B. Ask students to explain its meaning, and highlight the fact that it refers *only* to the past. Practise the pronunciation of these sentences by asking individual students to repeat them.

CONSOLIDATION

1. Draw two faces on either side of the board, labelling one *Clarissa* and the other *Donna.* Ask students to copy them. Explain that they were once friends. Dictate these sentences and ask the students to write them under the picture that they think they apply to.

   Clarissa is a top executive.
   Donna does charity work.
   She used to be rich.
   She lives in a luxury apartment.
   She lives in an African village.
   She never used to have money.
   She wears cheap clothes.
   She wears the latest fashions.
   She used to eat at the best restaurants.
   She usually eats at the best restaurants.
   She usually cooks for herself.
   She used to worry a lot.
   She worries all the time
   She is incredibly happy.

2. Allow students time to compare their answers in pairs. If necessary re-dictate any sentences that are causing problems. Then check the task. Note that Clarissa's story is a "rags-to-riches" one, while Donna's story is the opposite. The point of the task is to force students' attention of the "finished-ness" of *used to,* compared to the present-ness of *usually.* (The last three sentences can apply to either Clarissa or Donna, depending on the students' judgements as to whether wealth brings happiness or the reverse: this is something they might like to discuss.)

3. Ask learners, working in pairs or small groups, to make up more sentences about both Clarissa and Donna, using *used to* in at least some of them.

USE

1. Ask students to write some true and false sentences about themselves, at least two of which incorporate *used to* (as in the Discovery activity above).

2. In pairs or small groups, they take turns to read their sentences to one another, and to guess which sentences are true and which false.

LEVEL
Lower intermediate +

TIME
50 minutes

EXTRAS
Cassette recorder;
cassette of soft,
meditative music; model
text on OHP transparency

Section B

LEAD-IN ACTIVITIES
• A childhood incident
Recount a pleasant episode from your childhood/adolescence, for example:
When I was about six, my parents and I often went to a small mountain village for a holiday. We stayed on a farm. Close by, there was a clear stream. We often went there and I built dams with stones and made boats from bark ...

• A fantasy trip
1. Tell your students that you are going to take them on a fantasy trip. Ask them to close their eyes, sit comfortably and relax. Ask them to concentrate on their breathing for half a minute or so. Begin playing some meditative music. When you can sense that the whole class is relaxed, start like this:

Imagine you are standing close to a river. It's a wonderful morning, the sun is shining and everything is very quiet. There is a boat waiting for you. You get in and it gently takes you down a river, slowly and gently ... and after some time you realise that you have been in this place before. You are back at a time in your childhood, at a time when you were very happy. You row to the bank of the river and get out. Walk around and take all the time you need. You will meet all those people you spent that happy time with and you can do all those things again that you enjoyed.
(Pause for one or two minutes.)

And now slowly say good-bye to the people you met and walk back to your boat. You get into it and gently and slowly it takes you back to the place where you stepped into it You tie up the boat and slowly, very slowly, get out and walk up the riverbank. Keep walking, take your time and return to your chair in our classroom. When you open your eyes, you will remember everything you saw and you will be able to tell us about the time you just spent in your past.

2. Allow a little time for their 'return' to the classroom. When you are convinced that everyone is fully present, start asking your students questions about the situations they experienced. Avoid any impression of being nosey. If you feel that a student doesn't want to share, ask someone else. Usually most people are willing to talk about what they saw and felt, for example:
Student: I went for a picnic with my older sister and her boyfriend.
Teacher: Was it spring, or summer or autumn?
Student: Early summer, I think.
Teacher: Did you often go on picnics with your sister and her boyfriend?
Student: (laughing) Yes, I think my mother wanted me to go.

• Thinking back

1. Give the class a minute or two to think back again to a happy time in their childhood.

2. Write *I used to ...* on the board and ask each student to say a sentence relating to this childhood time. For example:

   I used to go hiking with my father a lot.

   I used to help my gran in the garden.

   I used to drive a tractor when I was only ten.

3. Correct the students' sentences if necessary.

4. Ask everyone to repeat someone else's sentence. Suggest they choose the sentence they liked best.

PRESENTATION OF MODEL TEXT

1. Present the text below on the OHP in the following way. Show your students the first line for about two seconds. Cover the line up and ask them to write it down. Proceed sentence by sentence. Allow about twenty seconds for the writing of each line.

2. Everyone checks with a neighbour and corrects any mistakes they notice.

3. Two or three students then read their texts out. Show them the text on the OHP for final correction.

Model text

I used to dream of expensive clothes

I used to dream of a holiday in Hawaii

I used to dream of a Porsche

and of parties under a silvery moon

but all I want right now

is a friend

who will listen to me.

TEXT CREATION

1. Write the following prompts on the board and tell your class that they can use *He, She* or *They* instead of I

   I used to dream _____

   I used to dream _____

   I used to dream _____

   and of _____

   but all I want right now

   is _____

   _____

2. The students write their own texts according to the model. Afterwards, ask four or five students to read out their texts.

The following two texts, written by fourteen-year-olds, very clearly reflect their concerns and problems at the time.

He used to dream of cars
he used to dream of computers
and he used to dream
of radios and television sets
but all he wants right now
is a family
who will listen to him.

I used to dream of birthday parties
I used to dream of going out until
twelve o'clock
I used to dream of holidays in Italy
and I used to dream of being a
champion at squash,
but all I want right right now
is to be healthy.

The following text was written by an advanced student:

He used to dream of equality
he used to dream of prosperity for all
he used to dream of being admired by his people
and he used to dream of being remembered
a thousand years after his death.
But all it really needed
were courageous citizens
who toppled him from his throne.

Variation
If you work with adults you may want to use the following model text:

She used to dream
of a loving partner
she used to dream
of a man who would really listen to her
she used to dream
of going places
and of a never-ending dream time
together,
but all she wants right now
is someone to help with the washing up.

ACKNOWLEDGEMENTS
We adapted the fantasy trip from *The Possible Human* (Houston 1982).

1.8 I'D RATHER BE ... THAN ...

LEVEL
Lower intermediate +

TIME
40–60 minutes

Section A

AIMS:
– to review ways of expressing choice
– to introduce *I'd rather be .... than ...*

DISCOVERY

1. Draw a circle on the board and write in it the word *choice.* Draw four or five lines radiating from the circle, like the spokes of a wheel. Write the words *Front or back?* at the end of one of these spokes. Ask the students what situation this choice might apply to. Possible answers may include: 'in a car', 'in a bus', or 'at the cinema'. Then write *Aisle or window?* at the end of another spoke. This time the choice is limited to 'in a bus', or 'in a plane'. Elicit some other possible choices that an airline passenger might be offered, either before or during a flight, and write these on the board at the end of the free spokes. For example, *Smoking or non-smoking? Vegetarian or non-vegetarian? Chicken or fish? Tea or coffee? Pounds or euros?*

2. Elicit more fully formulated questions and answers to go with each of these pairs. For example, *Would you prefer X or Y? What would you prefer, X or Y?* and *I'd prefer X.* Teach the formula <u>*I'd rather have/sit/pay etc X.*</u> Write these expressions on the board.

3. Ask the students, working in pairs, to practise the different choices that are on the board, asking and answering questions, and using the different formulae. Assign one student in each pair the question-asking role, and the other the answering role. They then reverse roles. This also could take the form of a role play, with one student taking the role of the check-in clerk, and the other the customer.

CONSOLIDATION

1. Copy and distribute – or project – the following matching exercise. Ask students, working in pairs, to match the half sentences so that *all* the combinations make sense.

I'd rather arrive late	than watch this rubbish.
I'd rather eat baked beans	than here.
I'd rather turn it off	than miss the plane.
I'd rather be at home	than not at all.
I'd rather arrive early	than take the bus.
I'd rather walk	than nothing at all.

2. Check the answers, and then ask students to imagine situations in which the sentences might occur. Ask them to choose one situation and write a short dialogue (about six to eight lines) that incorporates the sentence. They can then read their dialogues aloud or perform them.

USE

1. Ask students to draw a triangle and ask them to write, at each point of the triangle, one or two word answers to these questions:

   Where would you rather be?
   Who would you rather be with?
   What would you rather be doing?

2. Group the students into pairs or groups of three. (Alternatively, and if there is room, the students can stand up and mingle). Ask them to look at each other's triangles, and to ask questions about them. You can demonstrate this by drawing a triangle of your own on the board and inviting questions. You can also write the questions on the board, and gradually erase them as the students are getting used to answering them. Useful questions are:

   Who's/Where's/What's this?
   What does this mean?
   Why would you rather be with him/her?; ... there?; ... doing that?

3. Ask individual students to report to the class any interesting information they have learned.

LEVEL
Lower intermediate +

TIME
40 minutes

EXTRAS
A few copies of the model text

Section B

LEAD-IN ACTIVITY
• **Vocabulary work**
1. Form groups of three or four.
2. On the board, write the following pairs of words:

knife – string	*apple – worm*
flag – pole	*candy – wrapper*
dictionary – word	*truck – hedgehog*
star – sky	

3. Ask each group to write down another fifteen pairs and to make one copy of their list.
4. Then ask them to pass one of their lists on, so that finally each group has two lists (their own and one from another group).

PRESENTATION OF MODEL TEXT
1. Fix a few copies of the model text on the walls round the class.

Model text
I'd rather be *the sea than a ship*
I'd rather be a kite than a plane
I'd rather be a path than a road
I'd rather be a cup than a plate
Yes I would
If I could.

2. Get your learners to stand up and go to one of the copies of the text. Tell them to memorise as much of it as possible.
3. Ask them to go back to their desks and individually note down the first line (or however much they can remember) of the text. Then they return to the text and try to memorise the next bit and so on.

TEXT CREATION
1. Ask your students to produce their own texts in groups, using the words from their two lists of word pairs. Ask them to follow the structure of the text they recently noted down. (One text per group.)
2. One member of each group then presents their text to the class.

Variation
1. Write the following on the board:

soft against hard / light against dark /
warm against cool / hot against cold!
individual against whole / nature against man-made things

Give one or two examples for each pair:
cushion – brick / sun – night /
summer – winter / fire – ice /
flower – meadow / tree – house

2. Ask everyone to write another text either using images from one pair only (eg, soft against hard) or using images from various pairs. If your group is fairly creative, suggest trying for a humorous text that rhymes. For example:

I'd rather be a seesaw than a cat
I'd rather be a horseshoe than a hat
I'd rather be a coat rack than a mat
I'd rather be a monster than a bat
Yes I would
If I could.

The following was written by a thirteen-year-old:
I'd rather be the sun than the moon
I'd rather be a pearl than an oyster
I'd rather be a ring than a finger
I'd rather be an angel than a devil
Yes, I would
If I could.

1.9 SUPERLATIVES

LEVEL
Elementary–lower
intermediate

TIME
40–60 minutes

Section A

AIM:
– to introduce superlative forms of adjectives.

DISCOVERY

1. Spell the following names and ask the students to write them down. As they do so, ask them to think what they all have in common:

   Nile
   Sahara
   cheetah
   Everest
   redwood
   China

2. In case the students haven't guessed, the names all represent "records". For example, the Nile is the *longest* river. Elicit sentences about the other items and write them on the board. For example:

   The Sahara is the biggest desert.
   The cheetah is the fastest land animal.
   Everest is the highest mountain.
   The redwood is the tallest tree.
   China is the most populous country.

3. Highlight the superlative form of the adjective by underlining each example. Draw attention to the use of *most* with the polysyllabic *populous*. Elicit superlative forms for *small, slow, short,* and for *expensive, beautiful, famous.*

CONSOLIDATION

1. Announce that students are to take part in an "anti-quiz". A normal quiz is one where the contestants provide answers to questions. In an anti-quiz, the contestants have to provide questions for answers. For example:

   Quiz person: *Sahara.*
   Contestant: *What is the largest desert in the world?*

2. Organise the class into groups of about four or five. (You can give the groups the names of local football teams.) Each group must prepare five or six answers and their matching questions, to ask other groups. You will need to monitor this preparation stage carefully, to make sure that the questions are accurate and fair.

3. When the groups are ready, they take turns to shout out an answer. The first group to correctly articulate the question gets a point. When all the "answers" have been "questioned", the group with the most points is declared the winner.

4. Write up one or two of the more interesting questions on the board, and use these to remind students of the form of the superlative.

USE

1. Write – or project – the following table on to the board:

What Who	is	the best the nicest the strangest the most boring the most interesting the funniest the saddest	person film book song place	you have ever	met seen read heard been to	?

2. Elicit questions based on this table. For example:

Who is the funniest person you have ever met?
What is the strangest place you have ever been to?

3. Organise the class into pairs or small groups. Ask students to take turns to ask their classmates questions based on this table. Afterwards they should be ready to report their most interesting findings to the class, using this model:

The most interesting person that X has ever met is …
The strangest place that Y has ever been to is …

LEVEL
Elementary–lower
intermediate

TIME
30 minutes

EXTRAS
Class sets of words
handouts; (optional)
model text on OHP
transparency; a few
bilingual dictionaries

Section B

LEAD-IN ACTIVITIES

• Noun study

1. Hand out a copy of the following words to each of your students and allow them fifteen seconds to study it.

butterfly	*snowman*	*rainbow*	*snowflake*
sports car	*helicopter*	*pizza*	*pilot*
teacher	*tiger*	*elephant*	*piano*
mineral	*diamond ring*	*wind*	*eagle*
friend	*flower*	*insect*	*knife*
river	*pudding*	*ice cream*	*policeman*
leaf	*fairy*	*witch*	*snake*
ball	*tennis racket*	*storybook*	*word*
shark	*rainbow*	*surfboard*	*cheesecake*

2. Ask them to put their papers face down on their desks.

• Noun collection

1. In pairs, students write down as many of the words as they can remember. Allow about two minutes for this.
2. Ask them to shout out the words. Write them on the board.

• Associations and dissociations

1. Ask each pair to choose one noun from the list and note down at least three adjectives that they associate with it, plus at least one adjective they think has nothing at all to do with it. Give a few examples:
   ball: red, big, lovely (associations) / *stupid* (disassociation)

2. Ask pairs to read out their words. Note them on the board in two different colours.

• Comparatives and superlatives

1. Next comes a quick-response exercise. One student starts by calling out a classmate's name and one of the adjectives from the board.
2. The student called has to quickly say the comparative and the superlative. If right, erase that adjective from the board. If not, leave it until someone else gets both the comparative and superlative correct.
3. Continue until all the adjectives on the board have been erased.

PRESENTATION OF MODEL TEXT
Display the following on OHP or poster paper.

Model text
The most colourful butterfly
the sweetest cheesecake
the most beautiful tiger
the smallest snowflake
the fattest caterpillar
and the most dangerous snowman.
These are what I would like to be.

TEXT CREATION
Students write their own texts using bilingual dictionaries.
The following text was written by a twelve-year-old in her second year of learning English.

The most expensive ring,
the softest teddy bear,
the nicest rainbow,
the most colourful surfboard,
the biggest pizza
and the nicest teacher.
These are what I would like to be.

1.10 COMPARISONS, *LOOK GOOD...*

LEVEL
Lower intermediate +

TIME
40–60 minutes

Section A

AIMS:
– to highlight comparative forms of adjectives
– to make comparisons using *than*.

DISCOVERY

1. Prepare six to eight pairs of names of local places or institutions, such as two local train stations, department stores, monuments, avenues, football teams, universities, parks, restaurants, tourist hotels, cinemas or theatres. Write one of each pair on either side of the board in a jumbled order, so that the pairs do not match. Draw lines that connect the pairs, but make these intertwine so that they form a kind of spaghetti-like maze. Here, for example, is the "maze" that Scott prepared for a class in Barcelona:

2. Ask learners to "join" the two ends of each line (i.e., the paired names) by making sentences that include both names. Some of these sentences are likely to be comparisons (although not necessarily correctly formed). If no comparisons are forthcoming, prompt learners by saying, for example, *Which is bigger – Ciutadella Park or Güell Park?*

3. Erase the "spaghetti" and, in its place, write one or two correctly reformulated comparative sentences so as to connect names on both sides of the board. Preferably, these should include an example of an *-er* comparative form (such as *bigger, older)* or a *more* comparative form, such as *more central, more expensive.* For example,

   Ciutadella Park is bigger than Güell Park.
   Passeig de Gràcia Station is more central than Sants Station.

   Highlight the comparative structures by underlining them and eliciting the rule, ie, one-syllable and many two-syllable adjectives take *-er;* polysyllabic adjectives take *more.*

4. Ask students, working in pairs, to "connect" other pairs in as many ways as possible, using comparative forms. Individual students can be asked to read their sentences out, and the rest of the class can decide if they agree or not.

CONSOLIDATION

1. Copy and distribute – or project – the following picture:

2. Dictate the following sentences, pausing between each one. Students have to work out the name of each dog: *Mitzi, Patsy, Moritz, Max, Foxy,* and *Poochy.* (You can change the names of the dogs to more familiar names if you like.) Allow students time to compare notes and, if necessary, read out some, or all, of the sentences again.

> *Mitzi is taller than both Patsy and Moritz.*
> *Patsy is darker than Max.*
> *Foxy is darker and taller than both Max and Moritz.*
> *Poochy is taller than Max and fatter than Mitzi.*
> *Moritz is longer than Max.*

3. Check the task, and if students are having difficulty, talk them through it. For example, "*Mitzi is taller than both Patsy and Moritz.* So, Mitzi must be one of the three tall dogs and Patsy and Moritz must be two of the three short dogs ...."

Note: the answers are – from left to right – Mitzi, Moritz, Max, Foxy, Patsy, Poochy.

4. Ask the students to mask the sentences they have written down, and to write four or five sentences comparing the different dogs. As an extra, you can ask them to make some of these sentences true and some false.

5. In pairs, they read their sentences to their partner, who decides if they are true or not.

USE

Ask learners to prepare their own "spaghetti mazes" (as in the Discovery activity), by writing, on opposing sides of a piece of paper, and connected by a maze of lines, the names of pairs of people, places and things that are important to them (such as *my elder brother – my younger brother; my street – the main street; French – English,* etc. In pairs or small groups, they take turns to ask and answer questions about each other's mazes. Here are two starter questions (which you can write on the board):

> *What's the connection between X and Y?*
> *How is X different from Y?*

LEVEL
Lower intermediate +

TIME
50 minutes

EXTRAS
A recording of soft,
meditative music

Section B

LEAD-IN ACTIVITIES

• Word collection

1. Write the following on the board:

   I'm very, very lovely?   *strawberry*

2. Ask your students to give you as many words as they can think of that go with either of these two stimuli. Ask your students to shout words to you, ask which stimulus they belong to and write the words in a halo around each stimulus.

• Focus on poems

1. Read out the poems A and B (below).
2. Ask everyone to close their eyes and listen as you read the poems a second time. Depending on the level of your class, you may want to explain some vocabulary beforehand. When we tried out the activity with twelve-year-olds in their second year of English, we pre-taught *leaves, dropped, freeze, soup tureen* and *lima bean.*

   When working with adults, we asked them to do a short visualisation exercise before we read out the poems:

   'Close your eyes and imagine you are standing in front of a mirror ... go closer and look into it... now you realise that you're getting younger and younger until you are about ten or twelve. Take your time and look very carefully at your reflection and then slowly, slowly step back from the mirror, say good-bye to your image and return to the here and now of our classroom.'

3. When you have finished, allow some seconds of silence for the poems to echo in the students' minds.
4. Then read them out again to a background of soft, meditative music.

   Poem A
   ME
   My nose is blue,
   My teeth are green,
   My face is like a soup tureen.
   I look just like a lima bean.
   I'm very, very lovely.
   My feet are far too short
   And long.
   My hands are left and right
   And wrong.
   My voice is like the hippo's song.
   I'm very, very,
   Very, very,
   Very, very
   Lovely?

Poem B
I liked growing.
That was nice.
The leaves were soft
The sun was hot.

I was warm and red and round
Then someone dropped me in a pot.
Being a strawberry isn't all pleasing.
This morning they put me into ice cream.
I'm freezing.

<small>(Both poems by Karla Kuskin, Dogs and Dragons/Trees and Dreams, Harper and Row 1980)</small>

5. Ask your students to call out more words for noting down on the board. Some will come up with words they remember from your reading, others may well suggest new words.

• Dictogloss

1. Tell your students that you are going to give them a dictation, but they are not allowed to note anything down before you have finished it. Tell them that you are going to read the text just twice. Their task – immediately after each dictation – is to jot down whatever they can remember, then get together with a partner and try to reconstruct the text. Allow about three minutes.
2. The students dictate the text back to you. You write it on the board. If no one gives the right wording or if the students' suggestions contain grammatical errors, elicit words and correct forms with mime and gesture. If you get more than one suggestion and all are equally good, say that all are possible but try to elicit the original word or form.

Dictogloss text
My earlobe is bigger than a strawberry,
my nose is longer than a carrot,
my feet are shorter than potatoes,

my hair is thicker than grass,
my fingers are like beans,
I look good
I smell good
– no wonder everybody likes me.

TEXT RECONSTRUCTION

1. Ask everyone to close their eyes.
2. Erase certain words from the text you have on the board (see skeleton text on p. 62).
3. Tell them to open their eyes and give you the missing words. Continue until they have reconstructed the text.

Skeleton text

My _____ _____ _____ than _____ _____,
my _____ _____ _____ than _____ _____,
my _____ _____ _____ than _____ _____
my _____ _____ _____ than _____ _____,
my _____ _____ like _____,
I _____ _____
I _____ _____
no wonder _____ _____ _____.

TEXT CREATION

1. Before you ask the students to create their own texts, you may want to collect and/or introduce words under the following headings: *parts of the body, adjectives, fruit, vegetables.*
2. Tell your students that they can also use *his* or *her* instead of *my* and that they need not stick to the topic area of the model text. They can also write about other topic areas such as 'my room', 'our classroom', 'my garden' or 'my pet'.

The following example was written by a twelve-year-old.

My head is bigger than a pumpkin.
My ears are bigger than a tennis ball.
My teeth are blacker than a chimney
sweep.
My shoes are bigger than an elephant's
feet.
My nose is thinner than asparagus.
My hair is bluer than the sky.
I look happy,
I look sad,
no wonder I'm the clown.

NEGATIVE + *WANT SOMEBODY TO ...*

LEVEL
Intermediate +

TIME
40–60 minutes

Section A

AIM:
- to highlight the verb pattern *(don't) want* + noun phrase + *to-* infinitive.

DISCOVERY

1. Prepare thirteen word-cards that, when mounted on the board, will be visible to all the class. Each card should display one of the following words, and these cards should be sequenced as follows:

I	*you*	*go*	*to*	*want*	
don't	*her*	*he*	*wants*		*them*
doesn't		*stay*	*they*		

As an alternative to cards (plus Blu-tack or similar adhesive) you can use post-it notes.

2. Stick the first card (*I*) onto the board. Hand the four successive cards (*you, go, to, want*), along with some pieces of adhesive, to different students and ask them to stick them on the board so as to make a sentence. Ask the rest of the class if the sentence is correct, and if it is not, correct it (ie, *I want you to go.*).

3. Hand out the next card (*don't*) to another student and ask the student to add it to the sentence. (This will involve making room for it by moving the other cards slightly.) Do the same with the next card (*her*); this time the student will need to remove one card (*you*) in order to replace it with the new one. Suggest that they form a column (*you, her*) of words that belong to the same "slot".

4. Continue in this way with the rest of the words. Allow the rest of the class to suggest where words should go, but provide guidance if students are in doubt. Eventually, the thirteen words should form the following table. (You can tidy it up by aligning items and adding lines):

I			you		
	(don't)	want	her		go
he				to	
	(doesn't)	wants	them		stay
they					

5. Ask students, working in pairs, to produce as many written sentences as they can from this table. To make it more competitive, you can set a time limit, and then see which group has produced the most (accurate!) sentences. Or you can set the groups a target of, say, twelve sentences (there are 48 possibilities in all!), and the first group to reach the target is the winner.

CONSOLIDATION

1. Copy and distribute (or project) the following signs, and ask students to match them with the sentences that come afterwards, which you should dictate:

1   2   3   4   5   6   7   8

We want you to fasten your seatbelts.
We don't want you to take photos.
We want you to wear a protective helmet.
We don't want you to play loud music.
We want you to turn right.
We don't want you to use your phone here.
We want you to throw your rubbish in the bin.
We don't want you to light fires.

2. Ask the students to design signs for some or all of these requests, which you can either dictate or write on the board:

We want you to admire the view.
We don't want you to throw bottles out the window.
We want you to talk in English.
We don't want your dog to foul the pavement.
We want you to have fun here!
We don't want you to cheat in tests.

USE

1. Copy the following table on to the board.

I (don't) want	my best friend my partner my parent(s) my child(ren) my boss my company my teacher my school my college my neighbours the government the world to ...	to ...

Ask the students to use the table to generate three or four sentences that are true for them. They should keep these a secret and write them on a slip of paper. Collect the slips of paper, shuffle them, choose one, and read it out. The rest of the class have to try and guess whose it is. Continue with more of the students' slips. Use the students' statements to provoke a discussion by asking, for example, *Why do you want them to do that? Does anyone else share that feeling?* etc.

LEVEL
Intermediate +

TIME
50–60 minutes

EXTRAS
(Optional) OHP or big
flash poster of stiff cards

Section B

PREPARATION
Write phrases (below) on an OHP transparency, a big flash poster or stiff cards.

LEAD-IN ACTIVITIES
• What I don't want
1. Ask your students to work in groups of three to five.
2. Give groups the following instructions.

Group A
You are younger brothers or sisters. Your older brothers or sisters often tell you to do things you don't like. What I want you to do is to write as many sentences as possible of the pattern, *I don't want them to....*
For example: *I don't want her/him/them to tell me that I am not old enough to do something.*

Group B
You are parents. Write down what you don't want your children to do. Your model sentence is, *We don't want you to ....*
For example: *We don't want you to get home later than ten.*

Group C
You are children. Write down what you don't want your parents to do. Your model sentence is, *I don't want them to. ...*
For example: *I don't want them to tell me how much money they spend on me.*

If you teach a large class, here are some more ideas for groups D and E.

Group D
You are an employer/a teacher. Think about your employees/students. Your model sentence is, *I don't want you to....*
For example: *I don't want you to be late.*

Group E
You are employees/students. Referring to your boss/teacher your model sentence is, *I don't want him/her to ....*
For example: *I don't want him/her to make jokes about the mistakes I make.*

3. When the groups have finished, collect what they have written, read out individual sentences and ask the groups to guess who the speakers are (eg, boss/parents).

• Look and remember
1. Show the following phrases very briefly to your learners. Tell them not to write anything down at this stage. (Concentration is often

highest when the students know that they have only a limited amount of time to study the words.) Ideally, show the phrases on an OHP and simply switch it off after a short period of time. Otherwise, use a big flash poster or stiff cards with the words on them.

Be polite	*work harder.*
Don't tell me to	*my things without asking.*
Don't use	*you feel like it.*
Interrupt me whenever	*to call me names.*
I don't want him	*than me.*
She is older	*please.*

2. Individually, the students write down as many phrases as they can remember and then pool their notes with a partner.
3. Ask them to repeat the chunks of language back to you while you copy them on the board.
4. Ask them to decide which phrases go together. Connect them by drawing lines on the board.

PRESENTATION OF MODEL TEXT

Model text
All right
she is two years older than me
but I don't want her to

call me 'little one',
I don't want her to
interrupt me
whenever she feels like it,
I don't want her to
use my things without asking
and I don't want her to
tell me to be polite.
Let her change first.

1. Write the first letters of each word of the model text on the board or on a poster. Invite students to guess the words. For example:
A ___ r ___
s __ i __ t __ y ___ o ___ t ___ m __

The length of the gaps should correspond roughly to the length of the words that fit in them. This will not only facilitate the students' guesswork, but will also make your board work neater.

2. When you have elicited the text, read it out again.
3. Before your students write their own texts you might want to elicit individual sentences and write them on the board/OHP. In the writing to follow, the pool of sentences below can serve as a source of ideas and phrases. For example:

I don't want him to listen to my cassettes.
I don't want them to check my exercise books.
I don't want her to buy pink nighties for me.

TEXT CREATION
Ask your students to write their own texts. Prompt, if necessary:
All right
he is ... / they are / my parents ... / she is six years younger than me.

The following texts are by students in their fourth year of English.

All right
she is my teacher,
but I don't want her to give me
such a lot of homework.
I don't want her to interrupt me
all the time.
And I don't want her to ask me
words that I don't know.
But otherwise she is O. K.

All right
they are my parents,
but I don't want them to come
into my room without asking,
I don't want them to read my letters,
I don't want them to laugh
at my friends,
I don't want them to check my homework,
all I want is to live my own life.

Variation
If you work with adults, you may want to use the following text:

All right
he's my boyfriend,
but I don't want him to
slurp his soup
I don't want him to
wear pink ties with polka dots
and I really don't want him to go on saying
'That's what my mother says'.
I want him to
buy some anti-dandruff shampoo
I want him to
use a different aftershave
and unless he does – that's it!

1.12 *DO YOU MIND* + OBJECT + *–ING ...*

LEVEL
Intermediate +

TIME
40–60 minutes

Section A

AIMS:
– to sensitise learners to the multiple uses of *mind*
– to highlight the pattern *mind* + object + *-ing.*

1. Draw a circle on the board and write the word *mind* in it. Draw lines radiating from the circle. Ask the students, working in pairs or small groups, to brainstorm expressions with *mind,* and to think of situations in which they would use them. Alternatively, allow them to consult a good learner's dictionary. Some example expressions are:

state of mind
peace of mind
change your mind
make up your mind
lose your mind
keep something in mind
be out of your mind
have something on your mind
take your mind off something
all in the mind
mind your own business
never mind
I don't mind
would you mind ...?
do you mind!
mind you

2. Hand out (or project) the following concordance lines with *mind*. Ask the students to classify the examples into three groups. As an extra clue, tell them that there are three lines in each group. If they still seem to be having trouble, tell them to look closely at the word that follows *mind*:

1 and she said "Do you **mind** if I park here?" At which point
2 minister if he would **mind** repeating the question. The
3 that some people don't **mind** paying more money for healthcare
4 in the window. I don't **mind** people complaining but I do mind
5 me and said "Would you **mind** closing the door?" I went and
6 tor, "I hope you don't **mind** me asking, but have you ever
7 to ask me would I **mind** if the children knew about Clara
8 said Toby. "Would you **mind** if I invited my personal trainer?" I
9 house!" "Do you really **mind** us living here?" said Jo, with a

Note: A concordance is a selection of examples – usually authentic - of a word or phrase in context. For ease of reference, and so that they can fit on one line, concordance lines are often less than whole sentences.

3. Check the task. The three patterns are:

mind + *if*-clause (lines 1, 7, 8)
mind + *-ing* (lines 2, 3 and 5)
mind + noun phrase + *-ing* (lines 4, 6, and 9)

4. Ask students, working in pairs, to create their own examples of each of the three patterns.

5. Write the best of these examples on the board.

CONSOLIDATION

1. Ask students to match the questions (in the left-hand column) with the responses (in the right-hand column).

Do you mind me using the phone?	Yes, I do. It keeps me awake at night.
Don't you mind that dog barking?	No, but I do. Go outside.
Would you mind my sister staying?	So long as it's nothing personal.
Does the baby mind me smoking?	No, but don't make any long-distance calls.
Do you mind me asking you a question?	Yes, it makes me feel uncomfortable.
Do you mind people staring at you?	No, but she'll have to sleep on the sofa.

2. Ask the students, working in pairs, to choose one of the question-answer pairs from the table, and to incorporate it into a dialogue of about eight to ten lines, which they should write, rehearse, and be prepared to perform to the class.

USE

1. Ask students, in pairs or small groups, to think of at least five questions that include the word *mind,* and to each write all of them on a piece of paper. For example, *Do you mind people staring at you? How do you achieve peace of mind? When did you last change your mind?*

2. Ask students to stand and circulate, asking their questions to one another and noting the answers that they are given. (They will need paper to write on and a book to support this.) If mingling is not possible, arrange the class so that the students are sitting with students who are not from their original groups. In this way they can ask their questions to at least two other new students.

3. Bring the class together and invite individual students to report on interesting things that other students have told them.

LEVEL
Intermediate +

TIME
60 minutes

EXTRAS
Class set of handouts of skeleton text

Section B

LEAD-IN ACTIVITIES
• **Make up your mind**
1. Present the following list:

Some people ...
talk about themselves all the time
don't listen when you talk to them
drive aggressively
never admit mistakes
have bad breath
bite their nails
make a noise by tapping their biro while you're talking to them
lose their things all the time
leave their things lying around
pick their nose in public
never keep appointments on time
don't keep promises
forget what has been agreed on
gossip a lot
smoke during meals
eat noisily
talk with their mouths full
are very fussy about their food
talk on the phone for ages
play music very loud on the beach/in the street
worry a lot
never look into your eyes when talking to you
wear dirty clothes
don't wash their hair regularly
use rude language
make dirty jokes
boast a lot
don't write legibly
make it very clear that they feel very important
put themselves down all the time

2. Tell your students to write down five things from the list under the heading *It annoys me if someone ...* and five things under the heading *I don't mind people ... ing. . ..* Give one or two examples for each list.

• **Group work**
1. Ask your students to discuss in groups of four what they find annoying and why, and also what things they don't mind. Get them to add whatever else they think should be in the list.
2. Ask each group to decide which three things they find most annoying of all. Allow time to reach a group consensus.

3. Ask a representative to report the group consensus to the class.
4. Ask if there is anybody who doesn't mind the behaviour that others find very annoying. If there are students who don't mind certain things, ask them for their reasons. For example:

Student 1: I don't mind people who are fussy about their food.
Teacher: Why's that?
Student 1: Because they might be on a diet or maybe they don't eat certain things for religious reasons.

PRESENTATION AND RECONSTRUCTION OF MODEL TEXT
Hand out copies of the following skeleton texts and ask your students to try to fill them in.

Skeleton text A
D _ y _ _ r _ _ _ _ _ m _ _ _ m _ s _ _ _ _ _ _ _ e _ _ _ _ S _ _ _ _ _ _ _
a _ a f _ _ _ _ _ _ _ m _ _ _ _?
D _ y _ _ r _ _ _ _ _ m _ _ _ m _ s _ _ _ _ _ _ _ t _ _ e _ _ _ _ _ _ _
t _ _ _ _ _ _ _ _ w _ _ _ m _ m _ _ _ _ b _ _ _?
D _ y _ _ r _ _ _ _ _ m _ _ _ m _ s _ _ _ _ _ _ l _ _ _ a c _ _ _ _ _ _?
D _ y _ _ r _ _ _ _ _ m _ _ _ m _ g _ _ _ _ _ _ d _ _ _ _ o _ _ _ i _ a
w _ _ _ _?
W _ _ _, t _ _ _ w _'_ _ h _ _ _ t _ s _ _ g _ _ _ –b _ _ b _ _ _ _ _ _
I d _ m _ _ _ i _ _ _ _ _ _ _ _ _ p _ _ _ _ _.

Skeleton text B
D _ y _ _ r _ _ _ _ _ m _ _ _ m _ b _ _ _ _ l _ _ _ o _ _ _ i _ a
w _ _ _ _?
D _ y _ _ r _ _ _ _ _ m _ _ _ m _ f _ _ _ _ _ _ _ _ _ m _ h _ _ _ _ _ _ _?
D _ y _ _ r _ _ _ _ _ m _ _ _ m _ t _ _ _ _ _ _ t _ m _ m _ _ _ _
w _ _ _ I'_ b _ _ _ _?
D _ y _ _ r _ _ _ _ _ m _ _ _ m _ s _ _ _ _ _ _ i _ t _ _ t _ _ _ _?
D _ y _ _ r _ _ _ _ _ m _ _ _ m _ s _ _ _ _ _ _ _ l _ _ _ _ _ _?
W _ _ _, t _ _ _ w _'_ _ h _ _ _ t _ s _ _ g _ _ _ –b _ _ b _ _ _ _ _ _
I d _ m _ _ _ n _ _ _ _ _ –m _ _ _ _ _ t _ _ _ _ _ _ _.

Text A (key)
Do you really mind me spending every Saturday at a football match?
Do you really mind me spending the evenings tinkering with my motor bike?
Do you really mind me smoking like a chimney?
Do you really mind me getting drunk once in a while?
Well, then we'll have to say good–bye because
I do mind intolerant people.

Text B (key)
Do you really mind my being late once in a while?
Do you really mind my forgetting my homework?
Do you really mind my talking to my mates when I'm bored?

Do you really mind my smoking in the toilet?
Do you really mind my skipping lessons?
Well, then we'll have to say good-bye because
I do mind narrow-minded teachers.

Variation
Write the texts on the board or on an OHP transparency. Avoid slackening the pace during the guessing process by giving more letters of the word to guess; by providing words that roughly mean the same; by using mime and gesture.

TEXT CREATION
The students write their own texts and then read them out loud or display them in the classroom.

1.13 *TO HAVE A TRY AT ... –ING*

LEVEL
Intermediate +

TIME
45–50 minutes

Section A

AIMS
- to review expressions of the type *have a* + noun
- to introduce *have a try at (doing something)*.

DISCOVERY

1. Dictate, or write on the board, the following sentences, and ask learners to say what they all have in common (ie, the verb *have)*:

   1. *I have two brothers and a sister.*
   2. *I have never been to Japan.*
   3. *I have to be home before midnight.*
   4. *Can you have a look at my computer?*

2. Now, ask them to identify and explain the different uses of *have*. i.e., in sentence 1, *have* is a main verb, meaning 'own, possess'. In sentence 2, *have* is an auxiliary verb, part of a present perfect construction. In sentence 3, *have (+ to)* is a modal verb, meaning obligation. Finally, in sentence 4, *have* is part of a verb + noun collocation, meaning, in this case 'look'. (This use of *have* is sometimes called *de-lexicalised,* since it has no real meaning of its own, and functions solely to support the noun phrase *a look).*

3. Draw a circle on the board and write *have* in the middle of it. Draw some lines radiating from the circle. Elicit more combinations of *have + a/an* + noun. For example,

   have a break
   have a bath
   have a drink
   have a walk
   have a laugh
   have a chat

   Point out that many of these combinations have related verbs, such as *to drink, to walk, to laugh,* which have a more general sense. You can show the difference like this:

   To keep fit, I <u>swim</u>. (= generally)
   I went to the pool, and <u>had a swim</u>. (an event, with a beginning and an end)

4. Add *have a try* to the combinations on the board, and elicit an example sentence from the students. If this is not possible, provide some examples. Eg:
   I had a try at waterskiing once, but it was too difficult.
   If you need to relax, why don't you have a try at yoga?

Write the examples on the board, and draw attention to the preposition (*at*) and the use of the *–ing* form (*waterskiing*) or the noun (*yoga*).

CONSOLIDATION

1. Copy and distribute – or project – the following concordance lines for *have* (see p. 68 for an explanation of *concordance*), and ask the students, working in pairs, to classify them.

1. libraries in Wales	**have**	been lending books to each other
2. when everybody knows I	**have**	a big car and am capable of driving
3. so the tourists would not	**have**	to travel too far to eat?
4. married in 1967. They	**have**	a son, John Barry, and a daughter, Joy
5. about pension schemes.	**Have**	a talk with your bank manager
6. As a business man I	**have**	to use the telephone constantly, from three
7. Let us, like the French,	**have**	outdoor cafes where we may relax,
8. and her husband	**have**	a new baby. Their mother is Mrs. Candice Als
9. delightful cafes where you can sit,	**have**	a drink or lunch, and watch
10. next door neighbours	**have**	returned from a round-the-world trip
11. against blood sports. We	**have**	no right to criticize them, as they
12. wood furnishings	**have**	never gone out of style in Scandinavian
13. He said: "You'll feel a lot better after you	**have**	a bath. Your feet
14. and all the residents	**have**	been invited. This is going to be a fun
15. The government will	**have**	to decide whether to let U.S. steel in or
16. and said, "May we	**have**	a word with you"? "I'm sorry. I've had a

2. Check the task, and challenge the students to complete the beginnings and/or endings of the lines to make complete sentences.
   (The lines can be grouped like this:
   have as main verb: 2, 4, 7, 8, 11; *have* as auxiliary verb: 1, 10, 12, 14; *have (to)* as modal verb meaning obligation: 3, 6, 15; "delexicalised" *have*: 5, 9, 13, 16.)

Note: you can ask students to search for their own examples on the internet. All they have to do is find a web-page with a lot of text on it, such as a news site, and then search the page for examples of *have* using the search tool.

USE

1. Write the following prompts on the board:

   Would you like to have a try at ....?
   Why/Why not?

2. Elicit some possible ways of continuing the first sentence – for example, *bungee jumping, going on a TV quiz show* ... Ask the students, individually, to think of other examples and write them down. Allow them to consult bilingual dictionaries if available.

3. Group the class into pairs or small groups. The students take turns to ask and answer questions, using the prompts in Step 1 and choosing items from their lists. Ask individual students to report to the class any interesting facts they have learned.

LEVEL
Intermediate +

TIME
30 minutes

EXTRAS
Class set of worksheet

Section B

LEAD-IN ACTIVITIES
• Things we'd love to have a try at
1. Raise the issue of things people would like to do but never get around to doing. Give one or two personal examples.
2. On the board/OHP write a short list of sentences referring to activities suitable for the age of your students. For example:

I'd love to have a try at playing golf.
I'd love to have a try at making a video film
I'd love to have a try at learning to dance / to cook / another foreign language.

3. Ask students to note down two things they would love to try doing.
4. Invite them to read their sentences out. Ask whether they think they will actually do these things. Move on to eliciting more general ideas of why some people never fulfil their dreams.

PRESENTATION OF MODEL TEXT
Read out the following text twice.

'I'd love to have a try at playing squash,
I'd love to have a try at doing jazz dance,
I'd love to have a try at cross-country skiing,
I'd love to have a try at judo,'
he said.

But he never had the time
because he spent all his time watching sport on TV.

TEXT CREATION
1. Hand out copies of the worksheet. Ask your students to write their own texts individually or in pairs. Encourage them to mention activities additional to those on the worksheet.
2. Ask individual students or pairs to read out their texts.

Worksheet

	learning to ...'
	taking part in ...'
'I'd love to have a try at	*writing a book ...'*
	building a ...'
	opening a ...'
	selling ...'

he /she / my friend / my father / my uncle / my sister / my boss /... said.
But he / she never ...
Because he / she ...

1.14 *TOO* + ADJECTIVE, IMPERATIVES

LEVEL
Elementary

TIME
40–60 minutes

Section A

AIMS
– to teach *too* + adjective in the context of physical actions
– to contrast *too* and *very.*

DISCOVERY
1. Ask one student to stand up and come forward. Say *Touch the board,* and as you do so, perform the action. Repeat the instruction, inviting the student to perform the action. Then say *Touch the desk* (or any other object that is near). Finally, point to the ceiling and say *Touch the ceiling.* When the student protests, say *No, of course you can't touch the ceiling. It's too high.* Repeat *It's too high* two or three times, pointing at the ceiling. Repeat this sequence with another student, and prompt the student to say, at the appropriate moment, *It's too high.*

2. Write something very small on the board, and ask the students to copy it. When they protest, ask them *Why?* Elicit the answer *It's too small.* Next, demonstrate the meaning of the verb *pick up* and ask a student to pick up a pen. Ask the same student to pick up the desk, and (assuming this is not possible) elicit the reason *It's too heavy.*

3. Write *It's too high/small/heavy* on the board.

CONSOLIDATION
1. Write a word in normal–sized script on the board, and ask students to copy it. Write another word in a much smaller – but visible – script on the board; students copy it. Finally, write a word in illegibly small script. Elicit *It's too small.* Point to the first word and ask *Is it small?* Students should reply *No.* Point to the second word, and ask, *Is it small?* The expected answer is *Yes.* Ask them *Is it too small?* The expected answer is *No.* Tell them, *It's small – in fact, it's very small – but it's not TOO small.* Finally, point at the third word and ask *Is it small? (Yes) Is it too small? (Yes).* Review this sequence again, by contrasting the second and third words: *This word is very small. This word is too small.*

2. Show the class the following pictures and sentences, and ask them to match each sentence with its picture.

   a. It's very heavy.
   b. It's too old.
   c. It's too loud.
   d. It's too heavy.
   e. It's very cold.
   f. It's very old.
   g. It's too cold.
   h. It's very loud.

3. Allow students to check their answers in pairs. Then check in open class. If students are not sure of the "rule", ask them – for each picture – *Is there a problem?* Where the answer is *yes*, the choice is *too*, rather than *very*.

USE

1. Write some physical action verbs on the board that students already know, or that you can easily demonstrate. For example, *touch, point (to), draw, write, open, shut, pick up, put down* ... If there is room in the class to move around, include verbs like *walk, stand up, sit down, jump (over),* etc.

2. Demonstrate the activity by asking individual students to perform actions. Include some actions that are impossible, such as *Pick up the bookcase.* Prompt students to say *No, it's too big.*

3. Ask students, individually, to write a list of six to eight instructions of the above type. They can make the instructions more complex by combining two or more verbs in one sentence, eg, *Draw a face, point to it, and write your name.* They should then take turns to read an instruction to their partner, who should perform the action – or give a reason why they can't.

LEVEL
Elementary

TIME
30–50 minutes

EXTRAS
(Optional) Class set of model text

Section B

LEAD-IN ACTIVITIES
• Carry out instructions

Choose a student and ask him/her to carry out (not merely mime) an action. Do this several times, sometimes using new vocabulary for actions. Mime the action if a student does not understand the vocabulary. (Your class will have more fun if some of your instructions are unexpected or unusual.) For example:

Maria, go to the board.
(Maria goes to the board)
Take a piece of blue chalk.
(She takes a piece of blue chalk)
Draw a circle.
(She draws a circle)
Thank you, Maria, sit down.
(She sits down).

Françoise, come up front.
(She comes up.)
Take a piece of red chalk.
Put it in your left hand.
Draw a mouth in the circle.

Here is a routine we have used with seven-year-old children in one of their very first EFL classes, much to their enjoyment.

Take your pencil case.
Put it on your head.
Stand up.
Hands up.
Hands down.
Turn round.
Look down and catch it.

Depending on the level of your learners, they might enjoy preparing their own instructions individually or in small groups and then giving them to a partner.

PRESENTATION OF MODEL TEXT
1. Display or hand out copies of the following model text to your learners. Say each item and mime the action for each one.
2. Repeat. This time, ask your learners to do the actions with you.

Model text
Drink it up.
It's too hot.
Carry it home.
It's too heavy.
Write it down.
It's too difficult.
Take it off.
It's too cold.
Put it on.
It's too tight.

3. Repeat the text as a chant with the whole class.
4. Divide your class into two groups and get each group to chant every other line rhythmically.

Group A: Drink it up.
Group B: It's too hot.
Group A: Carry it home.   etc.

TEXT RECONSTRUCTION
1. Elicit the model text from your class by silently miming.
2. Lead a choral repetition of the text from memory. If the class get stuck or make mistakes, do not give them the language straight away. Use mime, gesture and key words to aid them.

TEXT CREATION
1. If you think your class will need prompts, put a list of actions and a list of adjectives on the board, for example:

Actions
Open   *the window*
                the door
                your schoolbag
Shut   *your mouth*
                your eyes
                the window
                the door
                your schoolbag
Buy   *a watch*
                some tea
Put on   *your hat*
Take off   *your coat*
Switch   *on the light*
                off
Pick up   *your bag*
                the ball

Adjectives
boring, funny, cold, hot, young, old, small, narrow, big, heavy, light, dark, bright, draughty, expensive, cheap, stuffy, full.

2. Ask your students to create their own texts based on the model text.

3. Ask individual students to read out the texts they have created while the rest of the class mimes the actions.

ACKNOWLEDGEMENTS
This lesson is in the tradition of Total Physical Response, a method developed by James Asher. You can get a good idea of how to work with TPR from his book *Learning Another Language Through Actions: The Complete Language Teacher's Guidebook* (2002).
The example, *Take your pencil* case..., comes from our coursebook for teaching English as a foreign language to primary school children.
Carolyn Graham's books (1978 and 1979) are an excellent source of *jazz chants*, some of which lend themselves well to TPR lessons.

1.15 ... FELT LIKE ... –ING

LEVEL
Intermediate +

TIME
40 minutes

Section A

AIM:
– to teach *feel like + –ing*.

DISCOVERY

1. On the board, draw a stick figure at work at a computer, with a thought bubble in which there is a stick figure swimming (see illustration).

2. Elicit ideas as to what the picture represents. Say: *He feels like going for a swim.* Repeat this two or three times, and ask individual students to repeat it. Write the sentence on the board.

3. Erase the content of the thought bubble, and replace it with a picture of a TV set. Elicit, repeat, drill, and write: *He feels like watching TV.*

4. Elicit further ideas from the students as to what the person feels like doing. You could even ask individual students to come and draw in the thought bubble a visual prompt which the others have to turn into a sentence with *He feels like ...*

5. Elicit the past tense form of the sentence: *He felt like going for a swim.* Write this on the board.

CONSOLIDATION

1. Copy and distribute these sentences and ask students to match the two halves of each sentence, so that all the sentences are plausible. Alternatively, the sentences can be copied and cut up, so that each student has a slip of paper with one half of a sentence on it. Students must then stand and circulate, repeating their sentence fragment, until they have found their "other half", and no two students are left with an unlikely combination.

When I saw the little kitten	I felt like walking out.
When the film got violent	I felt like asking for my money back.
When I failed my driving test	I felt like jumping for joy.
When the rain stopped the match	I felt like taking it home.
When our team won	I felt like banging on the wall.
When the neighbours had a party	I felt like crying.

2. Ask the students to hide the sentences and then to write down as many sentences as they can remember, working in pairs or small groups. The group with the most correct sentences is the winner.

1.15 ... FELT LIKE ... –ING

USE

1. Ask individual students questions like *Have you ever felt like walking out of a movie? Have you ever felt like jumping for joy?* Ask follow-up questions in order to get more details, such as *Why? What happened? Why didn't you? What did you do?*

2. Ask students, individually, to formulate at least five of their own questions using this model:

   Have you ever felt like ... ing ... ?

3. In pairs or small groups they ask and answer each other's questions, asking follow-up questions in order to get more details. Invite individual students to report to the class on their conversations.

LEVEL
Intermediate +

TIME
50 minutes

EXTRAS
A skeleton of the model text on OHP transparency or poster paper, two slips of paper for each student

Section B

LEAD-IN ACTIVITIES

• Match the parts

1. Write I *felt like* ... on the board and in a box give the students possible endings as in the box. Tailor the endings you give to the language that you have taught so far.

> *hiding in a hole – slapping his/her face –*
> *having a huge meal – hugging him/her*
> *– running away – saying 'No' – saying I was sorry –*
> *joining him/her – offering him/her a drink*
> *– smiling – bursting out laughing –*
> *saying 'That was the last time ...'*

2. Give the students a series of sentence beginnings by dictation, by writing on the board, etc. For example:
   When he /she read out the poem ...
   When he /she asked me that stupid question ...
   When he /she stopped crying ...
   When he /she called me an idiot ...

3. Ask them to finish these sentence starters by adding first *I felt like* and then an ending from the box (orally or in writing).

• Make your choice

1. Clear your prompts off the board.
2. Ask everyone to repeat the one sentence they liked best. It does not matter if several students give the same sentence.

• Make your own sentence

1. Each student writes a new sentence following the same pattern on two slips of paper, for example:

> *When she asked me not to phone her any more,*

> *I felt like smashing the receiver.*

2. First collect the slips that start with *When* ... and then the ones starting with *I felt* ... Keep the stacks separate.
3. Hand them out to your students again so that each student gets one slip from each stack.
4. One after the other, the students read out their slips starting with *When* .... The others suggest possible endings. If no one suggests the original ending, the student who wrote it says what it was.

PRESENTATION AND RECONSTRUCTION OF MODEL TEXT

1. Display a skeleton version of the model text, which gives only the first letter of each word.

Model text
When she opened the window,
she felt like throwing gold–dust all over the buildings.
When she listened to the cars in the street,
she felt like turning them into panthers.
When she looked at her tiny garden,
she felt like changing it into a jungle.
And when she looked at herself in the mirror,
she felt like painting her face the
colours of the rainbow.

2. Ask the students to reconstruct the text. Help them by offering synonyms, opposites and by using mime, gesture, etc.
3. When they have reconstructed the text, ask your students to close their eyes. Read the text out to round things off.

TEXT CREATION

Students write their own texts. You might want to provide the following prompts on the board:

When ___ ___,
___ felt like ___ ing ___,
When ___ ___,
___ felt like ___ ing ___
___

1.16

HEAR ...

LEVEL
Lower intermediate +

TIME
40–60 minutes

Section A

AIMS:
– to teach *hear/see* + object + bare infinitive
– to use the present perfect.

DISCOVERY

1. Write the following sentence on the board, making sure that the words are well-spaced:

> I   heard   a seal   bark.

Ask the students to suggest a context in which someone might say this sentence (eg, a zoo).

2. Convert the sentence into the first line of a table, by adding lines and numbers:

1	2	3	4
I	heard	a seal	bark.

Students copy the table into their books.

3. Read out the following words or phrases, pausing between each one. As you do so, the students should write each word into the appropriate column of the table. Repeat words, if necessary, and check that the students understand the meaning of the words by – for example – eliciting a definition, example or translation.

a dog
growl
chase a cat
saw
a kangaroo
we
hop
howl
have never heard
a cow
jump over the moon
have never seen
a pig
fly

4. Ask students to compare their tables in pairs. Resolve any problems they may have had in correctly placing the words.

LRS: Somerset Coll...

5. Ask the students, working in pairs, to generate as many sentences as they can from their table. This can be turned into a competition with a time-limit (which group can produce the most sentences in three minutes?) or a race with no time-limit (which is the first group to produce 16 correct sentences?). Elicit some of the more interesting sentences.

CONSOLIDATION

1. Prepare eight to ten sentences of the following pattern, and write them very legibly on cards or slips of paper:

I	saw	[person] [animal]	action verb (+ preposition)	[person] [animal]

Example verbs/verb phrases include *hit, kiss, dance with, shout at, drive away with ...*

Example sentences might be: *I saw an elephant dance with a tiger. I saw a policeman shout at a mouse. I saw the Queen drive away with a clown.*

2. Organise the class into groups of about four or five students. In each group there should be a sheet of paper and a pencil or pen to draw with. Tell the class that the object of the game is to correctly guess the mystery sentences, each of which follows the pattern *I saw X do something to/with Y.*

3. One member from each group comes to the front of the class. These are the "artists". Show the artists the first of the sentences, making sure that none of the other (seated) students can see it. Each artist returns to their group and attempts to draw the sentence so that their fellow team-mates can correctly guess it. The artists are not allowed to speak or to write words. The first team who can shout out the correct, fully formulated, sentence gets a point.

4. Another member of each team takes a turn to be the artist, and these new artists are shown the next sentence. In this way the game continues until all the sentences have been used. The team with the most points wins.

5. When the game is over, the groups then write down each of the sentences, using their own drawings as reminders. They then take turns to read these out, and the teacher checks that these match the original sentences on the cards, by, for example, holding these up so all the class can see them.

USE

1. Ask students to create four or five sentences, individually or in pairs, following the pattern *Have you ever [seen/heard/watched/listened to] anyone do Y?* The sentences should be within the bounds of possibility. For example, *Have you ever seen anyone slip on a banana skin? Have you ever heard anyone play the bagpipes?*

2. Once they have created their sentences, they should then stand up and circulate, asking their questions to one another and noting the answers that they are given. (They will need paper to write on and a book to support this.)

3. Once they have collected their "data" they return to their seats and write it up in the form of sentences. You may need to provide a model on the board for these sentences. For example:

Gemma has seen someone slip on a banana skin.
No one has heard anyone play the bagpipes.

Ask individual students to read one or two of their sentences to the class, and comment on these.

LEVEL
Lower intermediate +

TIME
40 minutes

EXTRAS
Class set of comic strip handouts overleaf

Section B

LEAD-IN ACTIVITIES

• Collect words
1. Write *people, animals, things, actions* as headings on the board. Elicit a couple of examples for each category *(fireman, horse, calendar, to eat,* etc.) and write them in columns under the headings.
2. Ask your students to extend each column. Allow three to five minutes for them to do this on paper.
3. Ask them for their words and add them onto the board.

• Mime the action
1. Ask everyone to stand up and to carry out the following actions: *light a candle, brush your teeth, kick the ball, throw the dice, put on a hat, climb a palm tree,* etc.
2. They sit down and write two more actions on paper, using the words from their lists.
3. Get the class to stand up in a circle. One after the other, students tell the class to mime the actions they have written down. (Or, each student mimes his or her actions and the others guess them.)
4. Hand out copies of the comic strip below. Tell your class to describe the frames of the comic strip using the following pattern: *I saw a ladder dance rock 'n' roll.*
5. Each student reads their sentences out to the class.

NOTE
We found that both adult and younger learners were more attracted by a surreal model sentence like the one above, as opposed to something like *I saw my friend work at his computer.*

PRESENTATION OF MODEL TEXT

Read out the model text. As you read the last two lines, conspicuously cross your fingers.

Model text

I saw a chicken kick a lamp-post
I saw a cactus drive a car
I heard a penguin eat spaghetti
I saw a teacher break a window
I heard a policeman howl at the moon
I saw a tree jump over a fence
and I swear it is true
John saw it too.

TEXT CREATION

1. The students write their own texts in pairs. For John each substitutes their partner's name.
2. Text publication (see page 11).

Note

Depending on the level of your group, you might want to explain when the bare infinitive (instead of the *–ing* form) is used after *see* and *hear,* ie, to say that we heard or saw the complete action or event...

1.17 POSSESSIVE 'S / OF

LEVEL
Elementary – intermediate

TIME
40–60 minutes

Section A

AIMS:
– to highlight the use of the possessive 's
– to contrast the structure 'noun + 's with the structure 'noun + *of* + noun'.

DISCOVERY

1. Write up, or project, the following pairs of film titles, and ask learners to select the correct title (that is, the title of the film in English) from each pair:

The Rings' Lord	The Lord of the Rings
Sophie's Choice	The Choice of Sophie
The Lambs' Silence	The Silence of the Lambs
Bridget Jones' Diary	The Diary of Bridget Jones
The Living Dead's Night	Night of the Living Dead
Captain Corelli's Mandolin	The Mandolin of Captain Corelli
Harry Potter and the Fire's Goblet	Harry Potter and the Goblet of Fire
Harry Potter and the Sorcerer's Stone	Harry Potter and the Stone of the Sorcerer
The Worlds' War	The War of the Worlds
Ryan's Daughter	The Daughter of Ryan
Notre Dame's Hunchback	The Hunchback of Notre Dame
The French Lieutenant's Woman	The Woman of the French Lieutenant

2. Check the task in open class. The correct titles are:

The Lord of the Rings
Sophie's Choice
The Silence of the Lambs
Bridget Jones' Diary
Night of the Living Dead
Captain Corelli's Mandolin
Harry Potter and the Goblet of Fire
Harry Potter and the Sorcerer's Stone
The War of the Worlds
Ryan's Daughter
The Hunchback of Notre Dame
The French Lieutenant's Woman

Ask individuals if they have seen any of these films, and to comment on them by asking questions such as *Who was in it? Did you like it?*

3. Ask learners if they can detect a difference between the titles formed noun + 's with those formed noun + *of* + noun. (The first noun in the former pattern tend to refer to people, such as Sophie, Bridget Jones, the French Lieutenant). Point out that this is more a tendency than a rule, but that it would be very unusual to talk about Notre Dame's Hunchback, or The Rings' Lord.

CONSOLIDATION

1. Copy and distribute (or project) the following grid. As students, working in pairs, to use the grid to *invent* titles of films, choosing two items from anywhere in the grid. They can add articles (such as *the)* and they should choose between noun + *'s* and noun + *of* + noun constructions. They should also try to imagine what the film is about.

prisoner	diamond	soldier	Tibet	last battle	my brother
hair	lost treasure	dawn	eternity	Shanghai	knee
Budapest	Napoleon	dark shadow	island	detective	golden ring
prince	dreams	magician	monster	president	mystery
journey	year	tower	only child	my cousin	secret book
Patagonia	terror	victory	heart	Iolanthe	ice

2. Ask individual students for the name of a film and a brief summary of what it's about. For example:

It's called My Brother's Knee. It's about football. The brother was a footballer. He had an injury. When he was in hospital he met a nurse and they fell in love.

USE

Teach students to play a game called *I spy something [adjective]*, as in *I spy something blue/small/round* etc. First, they take turns to think of something in the room that is part of something – or belongs to someone. They then say *I spy something …* and add the appropriate adjective. Other students have to guess what it is by asking questions, including questions that use the pattern noun + *'s* or noun + *of* + noun. For example, *Is it the hand of the clock? Is it Claire's knee?* etc. They can play this in pairs, or small groups, or as a whole class.

LEVEL
Elementary – intermediate

TIME
30–40 minutes

EXTRAS
Class set of worksheets A, B and C

Section B

LEAD-IN ACTIVITY

• A guessing game

1. Tell your students that you are thinking of something red. Ask them to guess what it is. Allow only questions to which the answer can either be Yes or No.
2. The student who guesses correctly continues: *I'm thinking of something green* (or blue, etc.).

PRESENTATION OF MODEL TEXT

1. Hand out copies of worksheet A or write the texts on the board.
2. Ask your students to fill in the gaps in text A.
3. Have them read out their solutions.
4. After that, read out the text twice.
5. Proceed in the same way using text B.

WORKSHEET A

Text A
What's purple?
My sister's _____
my father's _____
the _____ of my _____
my new _____
and the _____
I'm not _____ to _____
on my _____ .

| car hair allowed eyeshade use cover |
| jeans diary dye |

Text B
What's blue?
The _____ and the ocean
our maths teacher's _____
the _____ of the fly
that _____ my _____
and the paper of your _____
I _____ in my _____ drawer.

| secret nose body keep letter sky |
| head circles |

Model text A
What's purple?
My sister's eyeshade
my father's car
the cover of my diary
my new jeans
and the dye
I'm not allowed to use
on my hair.

Model text B
What's blue?
The sky and the ocean
our maths teacher's nose
the body of the fly
that circles my head
and the paper of your letter
I keep in my secret drawer.

PRESENTATION OF ANOTHER MODEL TEXT
1. Form pairs.
2. Student A gets Worksheet C1 and student B, Worksheet C2. Student A dictates to B the words B needs and vice versa. They are not, however, allowed to look at their partner's worksheet.
3. When they have finished the dictation, they compare their texts.

WORKSHEET C1
What's pink?
Strawberry _____
the _____
I _____ for _____ birthday
my _____ friend's _____
and _____ cuddly _____
who _____ me
when _____ am _____

WORKSHEET C2
What's pink?
_____ ice cream
_____ cake
_____ had _____ my _____
_____ best _____ earrings
_____ the _____ mouse
_____ watches _____
_____ I _____ asleep.

Model text C
What's pink?
Strawberry ice cream
the cake
I had for my birthday
my best friend's earrings
and the cuddly mouse
who watches me
when I am asleep.

TEXT CREATION

1. Read out model texts A, B and C again. Before you read, ask your students to close their eyes and picture all the things you are reading about.

2. Ask them which text they like best. Encourage them to give reasons for their choice.
3. Then tell them to choose a colour and write their own text.
4. When they have finished, tell them to stick their texts on the walls of the classroom.
5. Every student should read as many texts as possible and give feedback if they like a certain text. If necessary, put up two or three posters with language they might need for this, for example:

I like your text because ...
Your text reminds me of ...
I really enjoyed reading your text.
I think your text is great.
It's a beautiful text.
I wish I could write such a text.
When I read your text I thought of ...
I'd like to have a copy of your text.
Your text made me feel happy/sad ...

Note
Although designed for elementary students, intermediate learners have also enjoyed this activity. Here is a text from an intermediate class.

What's black?
The frozen leg
of the soldier,
the burnt tree,
the seabird in the oil slick,
the river of poison
and the mushroom cloud
in the sky.

1.18 ADJECTIVES / ADVERBS

LEVEL
Lower intermediate

TIME
40–60 minutes

EXTRAS
(Optional) class set of handouts of yes/no questions; class set of handouts of skeleton text

Section A

AIMS:
– to highlight the form and use of some common adverbs
– to contrast adverbs and adjectives.

DISCOVERY

1. Write *good* and *well* on the board. Then write up the following sentence and ask the students to complete it, using *good* or *well*:

    He cooks (1) ___ and his food smells (2) ____.

2. Elicit other words that could fill each gap. Possible words might be: (1) *badly, carefully, carelessly;* (2) *bad, nice, delicious, awful, disgusting, tasteless,* etc.

3. Highlight the difference between the kind of words that go into the first slot, ie, adverbs, and the kind of words that go into the second slot, ie, adjectives.

4. In pairs, the students should then try and complete these sentences:

    She sings (1) _____   and her voice sounds (2) _____ .
    He paints (1) _____   and his paintings look (2) _____ .
    She teaches (1) _____   and her students feel (2) _____ .

CONSOLIDATION

1. Write the following adverbs and adjectives on the board, or dictate them:

    nice
    badly
    slowly
    slow
    wonderful
    loudly
    brightly
    difficult
    suddenly
    bad
    gently
    good
    unhappy
    happily

2. Divide the class into several groups. Assign a spokesperson to each group. Read the following text aloud, pausing where marked.

    It was a lovely day. The sun was shining [pause], a light breeze was blowing [pause] and the birds were singing [pause]. I walked [pause] down the street on my way to the station [pause]. Although the weather was [pause], I felt [pause]. I was worried because my work was going [pause] and my boss was [pause]. Then, standing on the station platform, I [pause] decided not to go to work [pause]. Instead, I caught the first train to the beach [pause]. Although the train was [pause], I didn't care. I was alone, happy, free, and I felt [pause].

At the pauses the groups have to quickly choose an adverb or adjective that would be appropriate at that point in the text. Their spokesperson should then shout it out. The first group to provide an appropriate word wins a point. Words can be "used" only once, so you should cross each word out once it has been correctly inserted into the text. If the pause occurs at a place where *no* adverb or adjective would be possible, the teams should shout *zero!* in order to gain a point. If they don't shout zero but instead say an adverb or an adjective, they lose one point.

An alternative – less noisy – version of this activity is simply to dictate the text, pausing as above, and allow the students, individually, to choose the appropriate adverb or adjective from the list and write it down. They can have time after the dictation to go back and amend their texts. Afterwards they can compare their completed texts in pairs.

A completed version of the text might look like this:

It was a lovely day. The sun was shining brightly, *a light breeze was blowing* gently *and the birds were singing* loudly. *I walked* slowly *down the street on my way to the station [zero]. Although the weather was* nice/wonderful *I felt* bad/unhappy. *I was worried because my work was going* badly *and my boss was* unhappy/difficult. *Then, standing on the station platform, I* suddenly *decided not to got to work [zero]. Instead, I caught the first train to the beach [zero]. Although the train was* slow, *I didn't care. I was alone, happy, free, and I felt* wonderful.

USE

1. Write the following sentence frames on the board:

   What makes you feel .....?
   What makes you react ....?

   Elicit words that could complete each frame, eg,

   What makes you feel sad/angry/happy/good?
   What makes you react angrily/loudly/impatiently/gently?

2. Ask the students to prepare questions to ask one another using these frames. They can do this in pairs, or small groups, or (if space allows) by standing up and circulating.

3. Ask individual students to report on some of their conversations.

LEVEL
Lower intermediate

TIME
50 minutes

EXTRAS
(Optional) A sheet of poster paper for text A; (optional) flash cards; one copy of jumbled text B per group of four; OHP transparency of flash cards fo text C; class set of gapped text D

Section B

PREPARATION

1. Copy a version of text A – in which only the first letters of each word are given – onto an OHP transparency (or poster paper).
2. Copy text C onto an OHP transparency or flashcards (one line per card).

PRESENTATION OF TEXT A

1. Read out text A three times. The first time, your students just listen. During the second reading they mime the actions with you. For the third reading they close their eyes and try to picture the situation. After the third reading, ask them questions about the person's appearance.

Text A
He plays the guitar beautifully
He dances well
He moves fast
He sings well
There is just one problem:
nobody listens.

2. Present text A (on poster paper or OHP). Remove the text after a minute. Ask your students to work in pairs and reconstruct the text.

PRESENTATION OF TEXT B

1. Form groups of four. Read out text B. Ask your students to listen while you mime the actions.
2. Tell them to close their eyes and visualise the situation while you read the text a second time.
3. Hand out copies of a jumbled version of the text. Ask the groups to put the sentences into the correct order.
4. When students have assembled the text, read your original again as a check.

Model text B
The big car moved silently down the road.
I quickly hid behind the bushes.
The car stopped and a man slowly got out.
The doorbell of the dark house rang loudly.
A man and a woman started to talk angrily.
Then a shot rang out suddenly.
I saw the man's hat gently rolling away.

Jumbled text B
The doorbell of the dark house rang loudly.
I saw the man's hat gently rolling away.
The car stopped and a man slowly got out.
The big car moved silently down the road.

Then a shot rang out suddenly.
I quickly hid behind the bushes.
A man and a woman started to talk angrily.

PRESENTATION OF TEXT C

1. Show your students each line of text C very briefly (on OHP or flash cards). Their task is to write each line down.
2. When they have finished, they check with their neighbours. Allow two minutes for this.
3. Read out the text twice. Then show it on the OHP (or display all your flash cards).

Text C
It smells good
It tastes great
It looks beautiful
It feels soft
It's my latest recipe:
Strawberry cake.

PRESENTATION OF TEXT D

1. Form pairs. Hand out copies of gapped text D.
2. When your students have filled in the gaps, they read out their solutions.
3. Finally, read out the model text.

Gapped text D
It looks _____
It smells _____
It feels _____
_____ what it is:
My _____ dog.

little	wonderful	guess	marvellous	good

Text D
It looks wonderful
It smells good
It feels marvellous
Guess what it is:
My little dog.

DISTINGUISHING BETWEEN ADJECTIVES AND ADVERBS

1. Draw the following grid and write in some adjectives and adverbs.

ADJECTIVE	ADVERB
good	beautifully
wonderful	fast

2. Read texts A–D out again and tell your students to shout 'Stop' when they think you've just read out an adjective or an adverb. As adjectives and adverbs are identified, write them down under the correct heading on the board. Ask students to write down from memory the sentence they like best. It must, however, contain one of the words from the grid.

3. Students read out their sentences.

TEXT CREATION

Now ask your students to create their own texts individually or in pairs. You may want to give them another example:

Text E

He chews slowly
He eats noisily
But he cooks well
And his food smells very, very good.

1.19 GERUND AFTER PREPOSITIONS

LEVEL
Intermediate +

TIME
40–60 minutes

Section A

AIM
– to focus on some common noun + *of* + *–ing* combinations.

DISCOVERY

1. Copy and distribute – or project – the following concordance lines (see p. 68 for an explanation of *concordance*). Ask the students, working together in pairs, to look for any patterns or regularities.

Mrs Smith who said she had no memory	**of**	hearing an explosion although she
of excess fluid in the bottom. One way	**of**	getting rid of this fluid is to
that the low pass rate may be a result	**of**	watching too much TV and of
by the residents who are in the habit	**of**	throwing their rubbish out the
teenage drunkenness is a consequence	**of**	lowering the minimum age at
make sure you don't fall into the trap	**of**	letting a perfect stranger into
help for people who suffer from fear	**of**	flying and who consequently
minister claims to have no knowledge	**of**	receiving a payment from Mr
an investment portfolio as a means	**of**	saving money for one's old age
why the chancellor said that the aim	**of**	increasing the lending rate was to
a game show. So, if you have a horror	**of**	seeing yourself on TV perhaps you
said the president has no intention	**of**	resigning and said that he would
in some cultures there is the custom	**of**	taking your shoes off before you
of the month. Don't make the mistake	**of**	forgetting to declare your income

2. Check the task in open class. The pattern common to all the lines is the combination noun + *of* + *–ing.* These are some of the most common nouns that occur in this construction.

3. Point out that the nouns can be paired according to their meaning. For example, *memory of* and *knowledge of* both relate to the mind. Ask the students to make six pairs out of the remaining twelve nouns. (These are: *way/means; result/consequence; habit/custom; trap/mistake; fear/horror; aim/intention.*)

CONSOLIDATION

1. Ask the students to mask the concordance lines from the previous stage, and distribute (or project) the following gapped version of the same lines. Working in pairs, they should try to restore each noun to its correct place. To make it easier, you could write up the nouns on the board, ie, *memory, knowledge, way, means, result, consequence, habit, custom, trap, mistake, fear, horror, aim, intention.*

Mrs Smith who said she had no ____	**of**	hearing an explosion although she
of excess fluid in the bottom. One __	**of**	getting rid of this fluid is to
that the low pass rate may be a ____	**of**	watching too much TV and of
by the residents who are in the ____	**of**	throwing their rubbish out the
teenage drunkenness is a _____	**of**	lowering the minimum age at
make sure you don't fall into the ___	**of**	letting a perfect stranger into
help for people who suffer from ___	**of**	flying and who consequently
minister claims to have no _____	**of**	receiving a payment from Mr
an investment portfolio as a ____	**of**	saving money for one's old age
why the chancellor said that the __	**of**	increasing the lending rate was to
a game show. So, if you have a ____	**of**	seeing yourself on TV perhaps you
said the president has no _____	**of**	resigning and said that he would
in some cultures there is the ____	**of**	taking your shoes off before you
of the month. Don't make the _____	**of**	forgetting to declare your income

USE

1. Write the following sentence frames on the board, or dictate them:

I'm in the habit of … but I'm not in the habit of …
I have a dim memory of … but I don't have any memory of …
I have no fear of … but I do have a slight fear of …
I've never made the mistake of … but I once made the mistake of …
I don't have any intention of … but I do have the intention of …

Ask students, working individually, to choose at least two of these frames and use them to write true sentences about themselves. Forewarn them that they should not write anything that they would not want to share. (Early finishers can choose a third sentence frame to fill.)

2. Put students into groups of three to five. Each student takes turns to read out one of their sentences. The other students have to ask them further questions about their statement.

3. Finally, ask a member of each group to report on some of the more interesting things that emerged from their conversation.

LEVEL
Intermediate +

TIME
60–80 minutes

EXTRAS
(Optional) class set of text C handout

Section B

The activity is not suitable for learners below the age of 15. Additionally, there should be a strong bond of trust among the members of the group. (For exercises to build trust in the language classroom, see Moskowitz 1978 and Davis and Rinvolucri 1990.)

LEAD-IN ACTIVITIES
• **Nina**
1. Read out text A.
2. Ask everyone to close their eyes and imagine what Nina looks like as you read the text again.
3. Invite your students to say what came to mind.

Text A

Nina, who is in her first year of college, decides to spend her Christmas vacation with her family, although it is hard for her to leave her boyfriend Mitch. 'She examined herself in mirrors all over the house: the speckled mirror in the bathroom, the little oval mirror in the upstairs hall, the long narrow glass over her parents' bulky, old-fashioned bureau. In every mirror she saw only herself. Nina Pudding Face. Her old disparaging name for herself, popped out like a jack-in-the-box. Wasn't it awful? Without Mitch at her elbow to tell her that he loved her, she fell right back into that old trap of disliking herself.'
Norma Fox Mazer, *Someone to Love*, Delacorte Press 1985 p.133

• **The teacher's story**
Tell a story about a time you felt small or unworthy because of something somebody else said, for example:

A long time ago when I was a student, I took part in an English language workshop over the weekend for rather advanced learners. We were sitting in a circle and the teacher was just about to begin, having introduced himself in a slight Northern accent. At that moment, a stocky man in his fifties, with glasses and wearing a suit asked, 'Is it Queen's English we are going to use in our conversation?' Our teacher was kind of startled and didn't quite know what to say. The effect of the man's sentence on the rest of the group was, however, devastating. Everybody seemed to be asking themselves whether the workshop was the right thing for them. I clearly remember feeling very bad about the level of my English and praying that the teacher would not pair me up with the man who had spoken. I later found out that most of the other participants had had the same feeling. We were very relieved when the man left after a couple of hours.

• **The students' stories**
1. Form groups of four.
2. Everyone thinks back to a situation in which they, or somebody else they know very well, felt small, miserable or unworthy because of something somebody else had said. They all take notes and then tell their stories in the group.

PRESENTATION OF MODEL TEXT

1. Write Gapped text B on the board and elicit the complete words.

Gapped text B
It was awful.
When she heard that word
she fell right back into that old trap
of d _____ h _____,
of f _____ g _____,
of w _____ to c _____ into a m _____ h _____,
of t _____ back what she had s _____.
She was her old self again.

2. Read out the full text.

Model text B
It was awful.
When she heard that word
she fell right back into that old trap
of disliking herself,
of feeling guilty,
of wanting to creep into a mouse hole,
of taking back what she had said.
She was her old self again.

TEXT CREATION

1. Say that the topic 'falling back into an old trap' need not be restricted to a feeling of unworthiness.

2. As another example, present text C (by reading it out loud, displaying it for a couple of minutes, etc.).

Text C
It was terrible.
When he saw all the food in front of him
he fell right back into that old trap
of wanting all of it,
of being afraid of not getting enough,
of stuffing himself,
of eating far more than he needed.
He was his old greedy self again.

3. Present skeleton text C. The students use it to write a text.

Skeleton text C
It was _____ .
When _____
_____ fell right back into that old trap
of _____,
of _____,
of _____,
of _____,
_____ was _____ old _____ self again.

4. Publication of texts (see p.11).

1.20 IT'S HIGH TIME ...

LEVEL
Intermediate +

TIME
45–50 minutes

Section A

AIM:
– to introduce the expression *it's (high/about) time* + past tense.

DISCOVERY

1. Say the sentence *It's time you went to bed* in the students' own language and ask them to tell you how to say this in English. If the students don't know, say the English equivalent two or three times and write it on the board.

   If the class is multi–lingual, present the following situation:

   Draw a stick figure of a young person watching TV, above which there is a clock on the wall that reads midnight. Draw a second person – a parent – standing adjacent and pointing at the clock, with a speech bubble. Ask students to tell you what is happening and then elicit what the parent is saying. If the students do not come up with the target sentence (ie, *It's time you went to bed*), say it two or three times and then write it on the board.

2. Draw attention to the past-tense form of the verb (*went*) and ask *Does this refer to the past or the present?* (Answer: the present). Point out that this use of the past is similar to the hypothetical past in sentences like *If I went to bed now, I wouldn't be able to sleep.*

3. Ask students to think of words that go before *time* (in *It's time ...*) to add emphasis. For example: *It's high time ... It's about time...*

4. Elicit sentences, using *it's (high/about) time ...,* for these situations:

   a. you think your friend should have a haircut
   b. you think your teacher should give the class a break
   c. you think your brother should tidy his room.

CONSOLIDATION

1. Ask students, working in pairs or groups of three, to write two or three short scenarios that lead up to someone saying *It's (high/about) time ....* Use the situation in the *Discovery* stage as an example:

   A boy is watching TV. It's late. His mother thinks he should go to bed. She says ...

2. The students exchange their situations with another group, and write the response for each situation, using *It's (high/about) time ....*

3. They return their responses to the original group for checking.

4. Ask individual students to read out example situations and responses.

USE

1. Draw five large concentric circles in the board. In the inner circle write *Me.* In the second innermost circle write *My family and friends.* In the next, write *My work/school.* In the next, write *My town/neighbourhood.* And, in the outermost circle, write *The World.*

2. Ask the students to think of *It's time ...* statements for each of these dimensions of their life. Demonstrate this by giving examples of your own. For example:

   (Me) It's time I had my watch fixed.
   (My family and friends) It's time John returned my bike.
   (My work) It's time they got a better video projector at work.
   etc.

3. Give students time to work on their circle diagrams individually, thinking of at least one statement for each dimension. Then organise them into pairs or small groups to exchange – and respond to – each other's statements.

4. In open class, ask individual students to report, and comment on, any similarities they found in their statements.

LEVEL
Intermediate +

TIME
50 minutes

EXTRAS
(Optional) OHP or class set of handouts

Section B

PREPARATION
Copy 20 sentences on an OHP transparency (or produce a class set of handouts).

LEAD-IN ACTIVITIES
• Who said this and who to?
1. Write the following sentence on the board, and ask your students who might have said it and to whom. Ask them to give you words that describe the speaker's feelings.
   It's high time you tidied up your room.
2. Do the same with the following additional sentences.
   It's about time you learned to do this more carefully. It's high time you learned to cook. It's about time you got here.

• Building sentences

1. Write *It's high time* and *It's about time* on the board. Give everyone about 20 seconds to look at a range of sentences like the following (on a worksheet, the board or OHP). Select your sentences with a view to your students' age.
   You ...
   ... learned to drive.
   ... did a bit of slimming.
   ... stopped making funny remarks.
   ... stopped nagging me.
   ... learned to listen.
   ... behaved yourself.
   ... cut down on alcohol.
   ... started to do some exercise.
   ... told him/her/them your opinion.
   ... sold your car.
   ... had the washing machine repaired.
   ... decorated the living room.
   ... bought some new clothes.
   ... called ...
   ... wrote to ...

2. Cover up the sentences (or tell your students to turn over the worksheets). Ask them to write down as many sentences as possible from memory.
3. Ask several students to read out the sentences they remember, starting each with *It's high time* or *It's about time.*
4. Have each of your students say which sentence they dislike most and ask them to imagine the situation in which the sentence was used. Get them to try to use the same tone of voice the speaker might have used in the situation in which the sentence was originally said.

TEXT CREATION

Write the skeleton text on the board. Ask your students to write their own texts.

Skeleton text
It's high time you _____
it's high time _____,
it's high time _____,
_____ keep(s) saying.
Thanks for the advice,
but it's my time
you're talking about
and I'll decide
when to move.

If your students feel like writing their own endings (for the last five lines), encourage them to do so.

If you decide to ask students to read their texts out loud, spend some time guiding them in rehearsal. The first lines ought to convey the nagging, the second part ought to be spoken in a clear, firm tone.

Here are some texts from students in their fourth year.

It's high time you helped me with the housework.
It's high time you tidied up your room.
It's high time you studied harder,
Mum keeps saying.
Mum, don't be angry. It's my life.
I'll do what you want,
but, please, stop nagging.

It's high time you stopped asking this sort of question.
It's high time you started thinking about your work.
It's high time you tidied up your room
and helped with the housework,
she keeps saying.
Thank you for the advice,
but it is my problem.
You can't tell me what to do
because I hate people
who know what's best for me.

1.21

I WONDER WHY ...

LEVEL
Intermediate +

TIME
40–60 minutes

Section A

AIM
– to focus on verbs that are followed by both *wh*-clauses and *if*-clauses.

DISCOVERY

1. Copy and distribute (or project) the following concordance lines to the students, and ask them to look for patterns, and to divide the lines into two groups. (See p. 68 for an explanation of *concordance.*)

a. parents should be able to	**decide where**	their children go to school. It
b. said Ellen. "The problem is, I don't	**know how long**	I've had them." The
c. we looked at each other. "I	**wonder if**	you have seen the papers," I said.
d. because some people simply don't	**care what**	they look like as long as
e. given it to Susan. "I can't	**remember if**	she paid me back." "Why don't
f. in the pub. Stephen was beginning to	**wonder why**	Sarah had invited him.
g. number 46. Anyway, you will soon	**know if**	you are lost because the street
h. a policeman. "Just try and	**remember what**	they were wearing." "I can't,
i. sitting in the kitchen. "I'll	**see if**	we can find a bigger one," said
j. it's your fault!" "I don't	**care if**	I never see you again," he shouted,
k. in the furniture section. I can't	**decide if**	I like the beige one better
l. if it needs lots of work. I can't	**see what**	advantage there is in buying

2. Check that task. Establish that all the verbs in bold are verbs of "thinking", and that these particular thinking verbs can be followed by clauses beginning with *wh*-words (*where, how long, what,* etc) and by clauses beginning with *if.* To make this clearer, you can distribute or project the following:

a. parents should be able to **decide where** their children go to school. It
k. in the furniture section. I can't **decide if** I like the beige one better

b. said Ellen. "The problem is, I don't **know how long** I've had them." The
g. number 46. Anyway, you will soon **know if** you are lost because the street

c. we looked at each other. "I **wonder if** you have seen the papers," I said.
f. in the pub. Stephen was beginning to **wonder why** Sarah had invited him.

d. because some people simply don't **care what** they look like as long as
j. it's your fault!" "I don't **care if** I never see you again," he shouted,

h. a policeman. "Just try and **remember what** they were wearing." "I can't,
e. given it to Susan. "I can't **remember if** she paid me back." "Why don't

l. if it needs lots of work. I can't **see what** advantage there is in buying
i. sitting in the kitchen. "I'll **see if** we can find a bigger one," said

CONSOLIDATION

1. Copy and distribute the following exercise. Explain to the students

that they have to place the word in the left-hand column in the correct place in the sentence. It's probably a good idea to do the first one or two with the whole class before putting them in pairs to continue. (Early finishers can devise some examples of their own.)

a.	where	Do you know the bus leaves from?
b.	is	I wonder what the time?
c.	if	I'll go and see they have arrived yet.
d.	I	I can't remember where put the keys.
e.	you	Have you decided when are leaving?
f.	it	I don't care how late is.
g.	what	I'm sorry, I've forgotten your name is.
h.	not	Now I understand why it's working.
i.	if	Sometimes I wonder everyone is crazy.
j.	don't	I care what you wear.

2. Check the task, either by re-grouping students so that they can compare their answers with a new partner, or in open class. Draw their attention to the word order in these *wh-* and *if-*clauses, ie, that it follows the word order of statements, not questions.

USE

1. Write the following list on the board:

Sometimes I wonder	where ...
I really don't care	when ...
I wish I could remember	what ...
If only I knew	who ...
	why ...
	how ...
	how long ...
	how much ...
	if ...

2. Ask the students to use the list to generate true sentences about themselves. They should write at least three of these onto separate slips of paper.
3. Collect and shuffle the slips. Organise the class into pairs or small groups. Re-distribute the slips amongst the groups, so that each group has at least four or five slips. The students should then read them to each other, and comment on them, eg, whether they agree, disagree, find it interesting, etc. Finally they should decide which statement they would choose to read aloud to the class.
4. Individuals from each group then read their chosen statement. If the person who originally wrote it wishes to "claim" it, they may. However, if they wish to remain anonymous, that is their right.

LEVEL
Intermediate +

TIME
20–30 minutes

EXTRAS
Photocopies of worksheets A and B, one copy for each pair of learners

Section B

PRESENTATION OF MODEL TEXT

1. Put your students into pairs and give one partner a copy of worksheet A, the other partner worksheet B.
2. Students A and B dictate the text to each other. A starts with *When I go*, B writes it down and then dictates *for a walk* to A, and so on.

WORKSHEET A
When I go _____ , I _____ where
_____ a book, _____ why
When I _____ , I wonder what
_____ the phone, _____ who
When I _____ growing up, _____ when.

WORKSHEET B
_____ for a walk, _____ wonder _____
When I read _____ , I wonder _____
_____ open a parcel, _____
When I answer _____ , I wonder _____
_____ think of _____ , I wonder _____ .

Model text
When I go for a walk, I wonder where
When I read a book, I wonder why
When I open a parcel, I wonder what
When I answer the phone, I wonder who
When I think of growing up, I wonder when.

TEXT CREATION

1. Write the following prompts on the board:

When I ..., I wonder	*why ...*
	what ...
	when ...
	where ...
	who ...

2. Ask your students to write their own texts based on the model.

Variation

If you work with adults, you may want to use the following model text:

When I look into the mirror, I wonder who
When I'm late again, I wonder why
When I think of my holiday, I wonder where
When I dream of a pay rise, I wonder when
When I glance at the TV page, I wonder what.

ACKNOWLEDGEMENTS
The model text, *When I go for a walk ...,* was created by Jenny Skillen during a workshop on creative grammar at Pilgrims in Canterbury.
We learnt the pair-dictation technique from *Dictation* (Davis and Rinvolucri 1988, pp. 70–74).

CHAPTER 2
TENSE, ASPECT AND VOICE

PRESENT PERFECT *HAVE YOU EVER ...?*

LEVEL
Lower intermediate +

TIME
40–50 minutes

Section A

AIMS
- to distinguish between the meaning of the Past Simple and the Present Perfect;
- to establish the use of the Present Perfect with *ever* to talk about experiences.

DISCOVERY
1. Draw the following on the board, or onto an overhead transparency:

Now, write the following two sentences on the board, or dictate them:

1. *Did you ever climb the Great Pyramid?*
2. *Have you ever climbed the Great Pyramid?*

Ask the students to decide which sentence (1 or 2) best fits the empty speech bubble in situation A, and which fits the empty speech bubble in situation B. They should be allowed to discuss their choices in pairs. Ask them to justify their answers. (The answer is: sentence 1 goes with situation A; sentence 2 with situation B.

2. Ask the students to identify the form of the verb in each case: *did you ever climb...?* and *have you ever climbed...?* (The first is past simple, the second is present perfect). Establish a "rule of thumb" for the present perfect, ie, that we use it to talk about things that have some connection with the present. The past simple, on the other hand, is disconnected from the present.

CONSOLIDATION
1. Draw two faces on the board, one on the left and one on the right, and ask the students to copy these into their books or on a sheet of paper. Tell the class that the person on the left is called Amos, that he was a famous explorer, and that he lived in the 15th century. The person on the right is called Brian, he is also an explorer, and he is 70 this year.

2. Dictate the following sentences. The students have to write them under the appropriate picture. (An alternative way of doing this is to give individuals the board-pen, and they come up and write the sentence on the board).

Amos was an explorer.
Brian is an explorer.
He went to many countries.
He has been to many countries.
He has been to the North Pole.
He went to Japan.
He has never been to the South Pole.
He has crossed the Gobi Desert.
He crossed the Sahara Desert.
He never explored in America.
He went to China three times.
He has been to India twice.
He has explored in six continents.

Check the task. If necessary, read some, or all, of the sentences again. Write the sentences on to the board in their appropriate place, and draw attention to the way the past simple is used to talk about Amos, but the present perfect is used to talk about Brian. Remind the students of the "rule of thumb" that was established earlier. (Note also the use of *has been to* rather than *has gone to* to talk about places you have travelled to and back from).

3. Organise the class into groups of three or four. Ask students to imagine that they are going to interview Brian. How many questions beginning *Have you ever....?* can they think of in five minutes!

USE

1. In pairs, students ask and answer *true* questions with *Have you ever...?* They then each report their partner's answers to the class. Alternatively, they work in small groups and prepare questions to ask their classmates. They then stand up and walk around, asking their questions and noting down the answers. They then return to their original groups to collate their answers and produce a report. For example: *Nine students have eaten raw fish. Two students have seen a ghost....*

LEVEL
Lower intermediate +

TIME
Two lessons of 40
minutes each

EXTRAS
Cards or sticky labels;
two different coloured
pens; class set of
jumbled texts A and B

Section B

Lesson one
LEAD-IN ACTIVITIES
• **Sentences from back to back**
1. Write each phrase below on one card (or sticky label). Write some
   phrases in one colour of pen and the rest in another.
2. Stick/pin a label/card on each student's back.
3. Ask the students to walk round silently looking at the labels on
   their classmates' backs. Mentally, they try to build and remember
   as many sentences as possible. They are *not* allowed to take notes.

Red pen
I'd like to...
I wouldn't like to...
It must be interesting to...
It must be fun to...
It must be exciting to...
It must be boring to...
It must be difficult to...

Blue pen
cross the Atlantic on a yacht.
go to the disco three times a week.
have more time for yourself.
climb Mount Everest.
go on a bike tour to India.
have a teacher you can talk to about everything.
have a chimpanzee as a pet.
be ten years older.
be a cook in a famous restaurant.
travel to foreign countries.
be able to talk to animals.
see a ghost.
hunt for treasure.
write for a newspaper.
be a pop star.
be a curator in a museum.

• **Memory**
1. Ask your learners to write down individually as many of their sentences as they can remember and to do so under two headings:

   Things that are true   *Things that are not true*
   for me   *for me*

2. Divide your class into groups of about four and ask them to read
   their sentences out to each other. Allow time for students to talk
   about each others' sentences.

• Telling lies and telling the truth
1. The students work in different groups of four. Tell them to write down six sentences about themselves. Each of the sentences should either start with *I'd like to ...* or *I wouldn't like to ...* Some should be lies.
2. One by one the group members read out their sentences. The others listen and take notes about sentences they think are lies.
3. They then comment on what they think was true and what was a lie. This process is repeated until everybody has had their turn.

Lesson two
PRESENTATION OF MODEL TEXTS
1. Give everyone a copy of the worksheet below. Tell them to swap words between texts A and B so that the texts become meaningful. You might want to help them by underlining the parts that have been jumbled up.

WORKSHEET
Text A
Have you ever been away to an
expensive restaurant?
Have you ever dressed up awake all night?
Have you ever found to give a speech
at a friend's birthday party?
I haven't, but I think I'd like to.

Text B
Have you ever stayed as a clown?
Have you ever been invited from home?
Have you ever been asked a shooting
star in a swimming pool?
I haven't and I don't think I would like to.

2. Get one learner to read out their solution. Ask the others what they think about it. Read out the original texts.

Model text A
Have you ever been away from home?
Have you ever dressed up as a clown?
Have you ever found a shooting star in
a swimming pool?
I haven't, but I think I'd like to.

Model text B
Have you ever stayed awake all night?
Have you ever been invited to an
expensive restaurant?
Have you ever been asked to give a speech
at a friend's birthday party?
I haven't and I don't think I would like to.

TEXT CREATION

1. Ask your learners to write their own texts. In a lower level class, it might help to write the following prompts on the board:

   Have you ever...?
   Have you ever...?
   Have you ever...?

   I haven't, but I think I'd like to.
   I haven't, and I don't think I'd like to.

Variation of the lead-in

Instead of sticking the cards on students' backs stick them on the walls. Tell your students to stand up. Give them three minutes to find as many meaningful sentences as possible. Then tell them to sit down and write these down from memory.

Here are texts written by thirteen-year-old students in their third year of English.

Have you ever met Tina Turner?
Have you ever travelled to New York?
Have you ever interviewed a football star?
I haven't but I think I'd like to.

Have you ever seen a green dog?
Have you ever bitten the neighbour's dog?
Have you ever been a teacher?
I haven't and I don't think I'd like to.

2.2 PRESENT PERFECT CONTINUOUS

LEVEL
Intermediate +

TIME
45–50 minutes

Section A

AIM
– to introduce the present perfect continuous

DISCOVERY
1. Draw two sketches, one showing the beginning of a process, and the other showing the process some time later. For example, draw the stick figure of a person standing at a bus stop, and a clock that reads 5 o'clock. Elicit the sentence: *She's waiting for a bus.* Ask: *When did she start waiting?* (Answer: *5 o'clock*). Draw a second sketch of the same person at the same bus stop, but this time the clock reads 5.30. Elicit the sentence: *She's still waiting for the bus.* Ask: *How long has she been waiting now?* (Answer: *thirty minutes; half an hour*). Ask for a full sentence: *She has been waiting for thirty minutes.* Ask individuals to repeat this, and write it on the board. (Note: at this point, the contrast between *for thirty minutes* and *since 5 o'clock* is avoided, so as not to confuse matters, unless a student specifically asks.)

2. Read or dictate the following situations, and ask for sentences that fit the model sentence. (*She has been waiting for thirty minutes.*) Students can either volunteer the sentences in open class, or you can ask them to write them down, then compare in pairs, before checking in open class.

   a. Barry started reading a book at midnight. It is now three in the morning. So, he... *(has been reading for three hours).*
   b. Eva finished school and started working at the beginning of March. It is now the end of July. So, she ...*(has been working for five months).*
   c. Terry and Kim first met and started living together seven years ago. They are still living together. So, they....*(have been living together for seven years).*

CONSOLIDATION
1. Reverse the process of the previous activity. That is, give the students the *last line* of a short situation, and challenge them to reconstruct the situation, working in pairs or small groups. To start with, dictate the following sentences:

   a. He has been looking for them for two hours now.
   b. They have been dreaming of one for ten years now.
   c. She has been thinking about it for the last ten minutes.
   d. We have been expecting it to happen all day.
   e. I have been feeling this way all my life.

2. In pairs or small groups, they write their situations (of about three or four sentences) and then exchange with other groups. Monitor

the writing process, making sure that the situations that the students describe *continue into present time.*

3. Ask for volunteers to read out some of the more imaginative situations.

USE

1. Draw a sign or symbol on the board that represents an ongoing leisure activity or wish in your life. For example, it may be a Chinese character (to represent *I've been learning Chinese,* or *I've been wanting to learn Chinese).* Or it may be musical notation, or a paintbrush, or a book, or a country's flag, or a tennis racket. Ask the students to guess what your activity or wish is, by writing the following question frames on the board:

   Have you been (doing X)?
   Have you been wanting (to do X)?

2. When they have correctly guessed (or when you have told them), ask them to ask you *how long,* by writing these question frames on the board:

   How long have you been (doing X)?
   How long have you been wanting (to do X)?

3. Having demonstrated the activity, ask the students to do the same, ie, to think of a sign or symbol that represents an ongoing leisure activity or wish. They should draw this on a piece of paper. (A good idea is to have post-its available: they can then stick these on their chests, or even their foreheads!)

4. Ask the students to stand-up and circulate, asking and answering questions about each other's symbols.

5. At the end of the activity, ask if any students found someone with the same leisure activity and/or wish.

LEVEL
Intermediate +

TIME
40 minutes

EXTRAS
Handouts of the worksheet, cut up line by line; (optional) class set of model text A

Section B

PREPARATION
Make enough copies of the worksheet below for each student to have one line. Cut the worksheets into strips to distribute individually.

PRESENTATION OF MODEL TEXT
1. Ask your students to form groups of six.
2. Hand out a different line of the worksheet to each student in a group. Ask them to put the words in the strip into the correct order.
3. After the sentences are finished, the groups should use them to construct a meaningful text. Tell each group to stand in a line: the student with the first line of the text stands first, the one with the second next and so on. Then ask them to read out the words on their strips, one after the other. If there is not enough space for several groups to work simultaneously, ask two/three students to share one strip.

WORKSHEET
this/with/for/I/been/have/idea/carrying/me/years/around
it/I/been/have/of/dreaming/small/I/since/was
thought/over/I/at least/a thousand/have/it/times
think/one/and/going to/fulfil/am/day/I/I/my/dream:
own/book/little/my/to write
of/with/lots/stories/fancy/it/in.

Variation
In weaker groups hand out strips of words unjumbled.

RECONSTRUCTION OF MODEL TEXT
1. Give everyone a copy of the model text or present it on the OHP. Get your students to memorise the text by reading it silently to themselves line by line.

Model text
I have been carrying this idea around with me for years
I have been dreaming of it since I was small.
I have thought it over at least a thousand times
and one day I think I am going to fulfil my dream:
to write my own little book
with lots of fancy stories in it.

2. Ask everyone to cover their text and reconstruct it in writing with the help of the following prompts:

I have been...
have been...
since/for...,
and one day...:

3. Ask the students to compare what they have written with the original text.

TEXT CREATION

1. Tell the class about a long-time dream of yours. Ask everyone to work in pairs and to take it in turns to tell each other about a dream they have had for years.

2. Ask everyone to write their own texts about their dream(s) based on the structure of the model text. In addition to the prompts above, you could offer the following:

I have been waiting to/for...
I have been dreaming of...
I have been wanting to...
I have been hoping to...
I have been thinking to ...

Here is a student text:

I have been thinking about this problem for years.
I have been feeling this since my thirteenth birthday.
I have tried to bury it deep inside a thousand times
and on the first lovely day in spring
I think I am going to tell it to the others.
What?
That's my secret.

2.3 PRESENT TENSE FOR NARRATION

LEVEL
Intermediate +

TIME
45–50 minutes

Section A

AIM
– to introduce the narrative use of the present simple

DISCOVERY

1. Write the following sentence on the board, or project it, and ask the students to tell you what tense it is, and what *time* it refers to:

   He goes to a pharmacy.

   Students will (correctly) identify it as present simple and may say that it refers to a timeless present, or to an habitual present, etc.

2. Tell them you are going to supply more context to the sentence, and ask them to tell you if their original "hypothesis" still holds true. (If you are using an overhead transparency, you can reveal the context, having previously masked it.)

   There's this duck. One day, he goes to a pharmacy. He asks for some lip-salve. The pharmacist says...

   Students should now be able to tell you that the time reference is to the *past*, and that the text is a narrative, specifically, a joke. (They might like to guess the ending!) Point out that this use of the present simple is common in certain kinds of narratives, such as jokes, spoken anecdotes, and the summaries of the plots of films, plays, etc. The use of the present tense to describe past events is one instance of a mismatch between *tense* and *time*. (Other examples of this mismatch include the use of the past tense in sentences with present reference, such as *It's time you went to bed* – see 1.20.)

CONSOLIDATION

1. Copy and distribute the following jumbled text. Tell the students it consists of two texts that have been mixed together, although the order of the sentences within each text is correct. They have to separate out the two texts. They can do this by numbering the sentences 1 or 2, depending on which text it belongs to.

   Once upon a time, in the Kingdom of Dogs, there was a king. There's this man, and he goes into a bar with his dog. He was a big black dog, with a white stripe on his forehead. The barman says: You can't bring a dog in here. He was walking in the forest one day when he met a man. The man had a mouse. The dog had never seen a mouse before. So he says, I am blind and this is my guide dog. He said to the man, What manner of dog is this? The barman says, Ok, that's all right then. And the man said, it is a Mouse Dog, the rarest and smallest dog in the world. And so the man goes and sits down with his dog and enjoys a drink. The dog king was enchanted by this small dog. I must have this dog, he thought. Then another man comes into the bar. He also has a dog, a very small dog, a Chihuahua, in fact. It is hardly bigger than a mouse. So he said to the man, let me have your dog. And the first man calls him over, and says to him, Dogs aren't allowed in here. And the man said, On one condition. What is that? the dog asked. But if you tell the barman you are blind and that your dog is a guide dog, he will let you in. So the man goes to the bar with his dog. You must make the Mouse Dog your queen. You can't bring that dog in here, says the barman. Very well, said the dog king. But I am blind, and this is my guide dog, says the man. And he took the mouse back to his palace and made her his queen. Wait a minute, says the barman. Chihuahuas don't make guide dogs. And that is why, to this day, dogs don't chase mice. They gave me a Chihuahua? says the man, quick as a flash.

2. Ask individual students to take turns to read the two texts aloud. Ask the class to identify the *genre* of each text, that is, the type of text it is (ie, folk tale and joke), and to identify any characteristic features of these genres – such as, in the case of the folk tale, the use of *Once upon a time...* and the way the moral of the story is signalled: *And that is why...* Note also the use of the past tense for the folk tale, and the present tense for the joke.

USE

1. Ask each student to write the following two sentences at the top of a blank sheet of paper:

There's this penguin. One day he goes into a bar.

Ask them to write one sentence to continue the story. Having done that, they should pass the sheet on to the person on their immediate left. Each student then reads what is written and continues the story by adding another sentence. The process continues until the sheets of paper have each returned to their original "owner", who then has to write the ending to the story. To do this, of course, they will need to read the whole story through. If the class is large, it may be sufficient to let the story "end" when it reaches the twelfth student. Alternatively, the activity can be done in pairs, with students working together to create and add sentences, perhaps by repeatedly swapping papers.

2. Take some of the stories at random and read them aloud to the class. Alternatively, post them around the walls of the room, and let students stand up and read them. The stories will also be a useful source of errors: you can collect these and use them in subsequent classes in the form of a worksheet, where students have to work together to correct the anonymous errors.

Note: The joke in the Discovery section ends like this: *The pharmacist says, are you paying by credit card or cash? The duck says, no, just put it on my bill!*

LEVEL
Intermediate +

TIME
30–40 minutes

EXTRAS
(Optional) class set of jumbled text C

Section B

LEAD-IN ACTIVITIES
• Listening

1. Briefly explain/elicit what problem pages and agony aunts are. If anyone has never read a problem page, read an example out to them. Here is one from *Truth is Stranger...* (Landers 1968, pp.76–77). Read text A (both letters) slowly and make eye contact whenever you pause. Explain any words your students do not seem to understand.

> Text A
> *Dear Ann Landers*
> *My dad used to have a great build in his younger days. But a lot of beer has gone down the hatch since then and now he's sort of fat. Dad insists on sitting around the house in swimming trunks. When my friends come over I'm embarrassed. My mother doesn't like it either. Every now and then she'll say, 'Harold, go put on a robe'. But he pays no attention. My dad is wonderful and I love all 220 pounds of him, but do you think he should sit in the living room in swimming trunks when I have company? Ghandi's daughter*
>
> *Dear Daughter*
> *When your mother gives out with 'Harold, go put on a robe', Harold should go put on a robe. You wouldn't sit in the living room in your bathing suit when Dad entertains business friends, would you? Point this out to him. It might help.*

2. Tell your students that you are going to read out another agony letter but that it was not written by a person but by a thing. Read out text B, leaving out the line *I am a lamp-post.*
   Ask them to guess what the thing is. If necessary, write questions for the guessing game on the board. For example

   Is it made of... ?
   Can we see it in the classroom?
   Have people got it in their houses?

   Text B
   From a problem page

   Dear Maureen,
   I am a lamp-post.
   Every Saturday evening at five o'clock
   three boys
   wearing blue and white scarves
   blue and white hats
   waving their arms in the air
   and shouting,
   come my way.

Sometimes they kick me.
Sometimes they kiss me.
What should I do
to get them to make up their minds?
Yours bewilderedly,
Annie Onlight.

Michael Rosen, *Wouldn't You Like to Know,* Penguin Books, 1987, p. 75

3. When someone has guessed that it's a lamp–post, ask the class to guess why the lamp–post is writing a letter.

PRESENTATION OF MODEL TEXT

Present a jumbled version of text C on a worksheet or OHP. Ask students to number the lines in the correct order.

Jumbled text C
a tiny, old man and his big dog
What should I do?
when you enter the park.
and while the man looks away
Dear Maureen,
Yours miserably
come to the park
I'm an oak tree
the dog ...
Douglas Trim
the first on the right
Every day at about six o'clock
well, I'm sure you can imagine.

Model text C (key)
  6   *a tiny, old man and his big dog*
11   *What should I do?*
  4   *when you enter the park.*
  8   *and while the man looks away*
  1   *Dear Maureen,*
12   *Yours miserably*
  7   *come to the park*
  2   *I'm an oak tree*
  9   *the dog ...*
13   *Douglas Trim*
  3   *the first on the right*
  5   *Every day at about six o'clock*
10   *well, I'm sure you can imagine.*

TEXT CREATION

Ask your students to write, individually or in pairs, their own texts based on the model.

2.4 PRESENT PERFECT (COMPLETION)

LEVEL
Lower intermediate +

TIME
45–50 minutes

Section A

AIM

– to introduce the present perfect to talk about completed actions

DISCOVERY

1. Explain to the class that you are planning a holiday in Egypt (or any other country of your choice, but one that is appropriate for the plans that are listed below). Elicit some of the things you might need to do, in advance of the trip. Then show them this list (either by writing it on the board, or projecting it):

   1 *book the tickets* ✓
   2 *collect the tickets*
   3 *apply for a visa* ✓
   4 *order dollars* ✓
   5 *reserve a hotel room* ✓
   6 *buy a guidebook*
   7 *pack*

2. Tell them that you made this list a week ago, and the items that are ticked (✓) are done or completed. Elicit sentences (using *you*) and reformulate them (using *I*). For example,

   You've booked the tickets.
   Yes, I've booked the tickets. That's done.

   You've applied for a visa.
   Yes, I've applied for a visa. That's done.
   etc.

3. Do the same for the non–completed actions, ie,

   You haven't collected the tickets.
   No, I haven't collected the tickets yet. But I will.

   You haven't bought a guidebook.
   No, I haven't bought a guidebook yet. But I will.

4. Write some example sentences – both affirmative and negative – on the board. Draw attention to the use of the present perfect to talk about completed actions, and where the focus is not on the *time* of completion, but the *fact* of completion.

CONSOLIDATION

1. Distribute or project the following pictures.

2. Ask the students to listen and write the name of each person under the appropriate picture. Read the following sentences at natural speed, with pauses between each one.

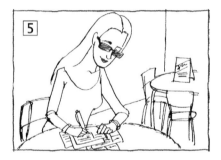

Ben has washed the dishes.
Brenda is having lunch.
Barry has baked a cake.
Brian is washing the dishes.
Betty has written five postcards.
Barney is baking a cake.
Belinda is writing five postcards.
Bridget has had lunch.

3. Give students time to compare their answers, and read the sentences again if requested. Finally, check the answers in open class.

4. In pairs, students write the full sentence for each picture.

USE
1. Ask the students to copy the following chart:

Things I do			
every day	once a week	once a month	once a year

Give some examples of how you would complete the chart for yourself. For example,

Things I do			
every day	once a week	once a month	once a year
walk the dog	*go to the gym*	*get paid*	*visit the dentist*

2. Ask students, individually, to do the same, filling in at least one item per column.

3. Point to your chart and elicit the question *Have you walked the dog today?* and answer *Yes, I have* or *No, not yet,* as appropriate. Do the same with the next item. Point out that the question for *go to (the gym* etc) is *Have you <u>been</u> to (the gym* etc) *this week?*

4. In pairs or small groups, students look at each other's charts and ask questions to find out how many activities have been completed or not.

5. Do a quick survey round the class to find out who has been the busiest, ie, who is the person with the most activities completed for today, this week, this month, and this year.

LEVEL
Lower intermediate +

TIME
30–40 minutes

EXTRAS
Bottle (optional)

Section B

LEAD-IN ACTIVITIES
• The teacher's favourite cocktail

1. Bring along to your class a bottle containing a brightly coloured liquid, or draw a bottle on the board with different coloured stars in it. Say that this is your favourite drink and that you got the recipe for it from a magician many years ago. Tell your students what the drink is called. Invent a fancy name, such as *Cosmic Cocktail.*

2. Before going further, decide on the ingredients. Do not tell your class what they are. Ask them to guess the ingredients. In order to make the guessing easier write the first letter of each ingredient on the board like this (but without the answers).

a bit of the	m _ _ _ _ w _ _	(milky way)
a bit of a	c _ _ _ _	(comet)
bits of	s _ _ _ _	(stars)
three	g _ _ _ _ _ _ _	(galaxies)
some drops of	s _ _ _ w _ _ _ _	(salt water)
a spoonful of	h _ _ _ _	(honey)

Answer questions with *Yes* or *No* only.

PRESENTATION AND RECONSTRUCTION OF MODEL TEXT

1. Write the following model text on the board.

Model text
I have blended everything nicely.
a bit of the milky way,
a comet
several stars
and three galaxies.
I have added salt water
and honey
(I like it sweet you know).
I have boiled
it for half an hour
and stirred it carefully.
Maybe you would like to taste it:
my wonderful cosmic cocktail.

2. Give the class 30 seconds to study the text.
3. Then rub out everything except for the following:

I have _____ :
a bit of _____ ,
a _____
several _____
and three _____ .
I have _____

and _____
(I _____ *)*
I have _____
for _____
and _____ *.*
Maybe _____ *:*
my wonderful _____ *.*

4. Students try to write the full text in pairs. Read out the original once more and ask them to correct their versions of the text. Leave the prompts on the board. Your students might need them in the writing stage later on.

• **Collecting language**
1. Revise or teach the following verbs and noun phrases, so that your students will have a greater variety of language at their disposal in the writing stage. Write them on the board.

Verbs
to mix / to blend / to boil / to grind / to cut /
to add / to stir / to put in

Quantities
a litre of / a pint of / a kilogramme of /
a pound of / a packet of / a tin of / a bottle of /
a cup of/ a glass of/a piece of/
a spoonful of / a bit of / pieces of / some drops of

2. Give your class time to study the words on the board.
3. Revise the words by forming them without making a sound. The students have to guess the words from the movements of your lips.
4. Cover the words up and ask the students to remember as many as they can.

TEXT CREATION
Ask your students to create their own texts based on the model. Mention that if anyone decides to use time or order markers like *first, second, then,* they will have to shift to the past tense. Here is a text written by a student in the second year of English.

We have blended some western things:
pieces of cowboys
an old hat
and a gun.
We have added a cactus
and some sand.
We've ground some lassos
and saddles and stirred everything
carefully.
Maybe you would like to taste it:
our wonderful western cocktail.

2.5 PAST PASSIVE

LEVEL
Intermediate +

TIME
45–50 minutes

Section A

AIM
– to introduce the past passive

DISCOVERY
1. Write the following on the board:

   THE MYTHICAL TIMES

   Tell the students that this is the name of a newspaper, and then write some of the headlines from the newspaper, choosing myths and stories that will be familiar in your students' own culture. For example:

   Dragon killed by youth
   Man swallowed by whale
   Grandmother eaten by wolf
   Frog kissed by princess
   Twins nursed by wolf

2. Ask the students if they recognise any of these "news" stories. (In the case of the above headlines, the myths and legends they refer to are, respectively, George and the dragon, Jonah and the whale, Little Red Riding-Hood, the frog prince, and the legend of Romulus and Remus.)

3. Ask the students, working in pairs, to write the first sentence of each "news" story by expanding each headline, using this model:

   Yesterday a dragon was killed by a youth.

4. Write some of these sentences on the board, and use them to highlight the form of the past passive.

5. Assign different pairs one of the news stories each, and ask them to continue writing it, summarising the main events, and even adding a comment from a witness. For example:

   Yesterday a grandmother was eaten by a wolf. Eighty-year-old Vera Hood was alone in her house at the time, awaiting the arrival of her granddaughter, Red Riding-Hood. Apparently, the wolf entered without knocking and gobbled up the granny. He then disguised himself as the unfortunate old lady. On arrival, Little Red almost became the wolf's second victim. Fortunately, a quick-witted woodsman came to the rescue. "It was her big teeth that made me suspicious", commented Little Red.

CONSOLIDATION

1. Prepare eight to ten sentences of the following pattern, and write them very legibly on cards or slips of paper:

[An animal] [A person]	*was*	past participle	*by*	[an animal] [a person]

For example: *An elephant was swallowed by a snake; A hairdresser was frightened by a mouse; A lion was chased by a clown.*

2. Organise the class into groups of about four or five students. In each group there should be a sheet of paper and a pencil or pen to draw with. Tell the class that the object of the game is to correctly guess the mystery sentences, each of which follows the past passive pattern *(X was -ed by Y)*.

3. One member from each group comes to the front of the class. These are the "artists". Show the artists the first of the sentences, making sure that none of the other (seated) students can see it. Each artist returns to their group and attempts to draw the sentence so that their fellow team-mates can correctly guess it. The artists are not allowed to speak or to write words. The first team who can shout out the correct, fully formulated, sentence gets a point.

4. Another member of each team takes a turn to be the artist, and these new artists are shown the next sentence. In this way the game continues until all the sentences have been used. The team with the most points wins.

5. When the game is over, the groups then write down each of the sentences, using their own drawings as reminders. They then take turns to read these out, and the teacher checks that these match the original sentences on the cards, by, for example, holding these up so all the class can see them.

USE

1. Prepare three or four sentences about yourself, using the past passive. Some of the sentences should be true, and some false. For example,

Once I was mistaken for Jane Fonda.
Once I was bitten by a mongoose.
Once I was arrested for jaywalking.

2. Ask the students to guess which sentences are true and false. Once they have guessed, invite them to ask you more questions about the true stories. You can provide example sentences and write them on the board. For example:

When did that happen?
How did you feel?
What did you say?
etc.

3. Students then do the same. Individually, they compose their true/false sentences, using the past passive. In pairs or small groups they take turns to read their sentences aloud. Their classmates then try and guess which sentences are true. They then have a short conversation about the true stories. Finally, invite individual students to recount some of these stories to the whole class.

LEVEL
Intermediate +

TIME
40–50 minutes

EXTRAS
(Optional) OHP or two
large sheets of poster
paper; pen or stick

Section B

PREPARATION
Copy the picture puzzle and skeleton text onto (separate) OHP transparencies or large sheets of poster paper.

PRESENTATION OF MODEL TEXT
1. Display the picture puzzle below.

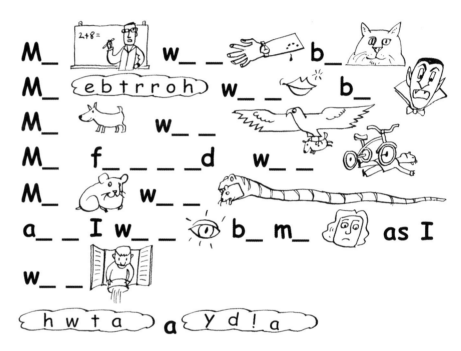

2. Remain silent for one or two minutes. Try to elicit words from the students. If someone guesses a word correctly, point to the corresponding picture/letter(s) in the puzzle and nod your head.
3. Point to the first line of the picture puzzle. Elicit the first line of the model text below and write it on the board. Proceed like this with all the other lines of the model text.

Model text
My biology teacher was bitten by a cat
My brother was kissed by a vampire
My dog was kidnapped by an eagle
My friend was run over by a tricycle
My hamster was eaten by a snake
and I was seen by my mother
as I was pouring a bowl
of tomato soup
out of the kitchen window.
What a day!

FIRST TEXT RECONSTRUCTION

1. Tell the students to rehearse the model text by reading it half out loud to themselves.
2. Form pairs. Remove the model text/switch off the OHP.
3. Ask the pairs to look at the picture puzzle and write the model text.
4. Re-form the class. Ask someone to come to the board.
5. Get the other students to dictate the text to the person at the board. Do not interfere, even if the text on the board is different from the original.
6. Form pairs again.
7. Display the skeleton text. Ask the pairs to check their texts against the text on the board and the skeleton text. Tell them to add to their texts and correct them. Do not interfere as long as your students do not get stuck. Allow about three minutes.
8. Display the full model text again. Get students to check and correct their version against it.

Skeleton text
M _ b _ _ _ _ _ _ t _ _ _ _ _ _ w _ _ b _ _ _ _ _ b _ a c _ _
M _ b _ _ _ _ _ _ w _ _ k _ _ _ _ _ b _ a v _ _ _ _ _ _
M _ d _ _ w _ _ k _ _ _ _ _ _ _ _ b _ a _ e _ _ _ _
M _ f _ _ _ _ _ w _ _ r _ _ o _ _ _ b _ a t _ _ _ _ _ _ _
M _ h _ _ _ _ _ _ w _ _ e _ _ _ _ b _ a s _ _ _ _
a _ _ I w _ _ s _ _ _ b _ m _ m _ _ _ _ _
a _ I w _ _ p _ _ _ _ _ _ a b _ _ _
o _ t _ _ _ _ _ s _ _ _
o _ _ o _ t _ _ k _ _ _ _ _ _ w _ _ _ _ _.
W _ _ _ a d _ _ !

SECOND TEXT RECONSTRUCTION

1. Ask your class to put their texts face down on their desks. Continue to display the skeleton text.
2. Lead a choral reconstruction of the text. Guide by moving a pen or stick at reading speed through the text.

THIRD TEXT RECONSTRUCTION

1. Now switch off the OHP/remove the text skeleton.
2. Lead another choral reconstruction of the text.

TEXT CREATION

Everyone writes their own texts. Allow about ten minutes.
The following text is by a thirteen-year-old in the third year of English.

My mother was bitten by a dog
My sister was bitten by a snake
My brother was thrown into a swimming pool
I was knocked down by a car
when I was crossing the street
My cousin was kissed by a budgie

and my boyfriend fell ill
when a pumpkin was dropped on his head.
What a day!

Extension

When you have corrected the students' texts, ask them to write a skeleton version of their text as homework. These student skeleton texts can then be redistributed and used for further practice.

Variation

If you work with adults, you may want to use the following text:
At the office
a door was slammed in my face
I was told several lies
and my new computer programme
was eaten by a virus.
In the pub
I was looked up and down
by all the men
and when I blew my top
I was politely asked to leave.
When I came home,
I found out that my phone had been disconnected
and there was no way
of sharing my anger
with anybody.

2.6 GOING TO

LEVEL
Elementary – lower intermediate

TIME
45–50 minutes

Section A

AIM
– to introduce *going to,* to talk about intentions

DISCOVERY

1. Assemble some objects on a flat surface – such as a table or desk – that is visible to all the students. If you have access to *cuisenaire rods*, these are ideal. But, if not, a collection of different coloured pens and books will do just as well. Items of plastic fruit (available from many department stores) also work well. Check that the students know the names and colours of the different objects. You may also want to check that they are familiar with some basic prepositions of place, such as *in, on, behind, next to, between, in front of,* etc.

2. Get the students' attention, and tell them to listen and watch closely. Announce what you plan to do. For example (if using cuisenaire rods):

   I'm going to take the red rod and put it on the desk. Then I'm going to take the green rod and put it near the red rod. Then I'm going to put the black rod between the green and red rods.

3. Perform the action that you described, and ask the students if you did it correctly.

4. Repeat this activity, using different routines (which can become increasingly more complicated), some of which you "get wrong". Allow the students to correct you.

5. Invite a volunteer to do the same. At this point, you may want to draw attention to the language you have been using to announce your plans. On the board write

   I'm going to take/put the X rod near/on/under etc *the Y rod.*

6. At the end of the activity, draw attention to the structure *going to,* and point out that it is used to talk about plans and intentions.

CONSOLIDATION

1. Copy and distribute the following matching activity. Ask students, working individually and then comparing in pairs, to match the plans (on the left) with the "evidence" (on the right).

Dan and Jackie are going to get married.	*They've already started looking for one.*
Arthur is going to retire next year.	*They've already booked their flight.*
Robin and Chris are going to buy a house.	*He's already told his boss.*
Cheryl is going to be a doctor.	*He's already got a publisher.*

Vivian and Terry are going to spend a week in the Maldives.
Darlene is going to start her own business.
James is going to write a novel.
Nick is going to learn Chinese.

He's already found a teacher.
They've already got the rings.
She's already got a name for it.
She's already graduated from medical school.

2. When you have checked the task, forewarn the students that you are going to test their memories. Let them study the information for half a minute, and then ask them to turn their papers over. Ask questions, such as:

Who's going to be a doctor?
What is Nick going to do?
etc.

You can turn this into a competition by organising the class into teams and allocating one point for each correct answer.

USE

1. Draw the following chart on the board:

	today	tomorrow	next week	next month
work/school				
free time				

Partly fill in the chart with notes that represent your plans. For example:

	today	tomorrow	next week	next month
work/school	*correct homework*		*staff meeting*	*conference*
free time		*movie*	*hairdresser*	

Ask students to use these notes to ask you about your plans. You can provide some useful questions, and write these on the board:

Are you going to see a movie tomorrow?
What are you going to see?
Who are you going to go with?
etc.

2. Ask students, working individually, to copy the chart and to make notes in the relevant boxes, according to plans they have made. They then exchange their charts with their neighbour, and ask and answer questions about it.

LEVEL
Elementary – lower
intermediate

TIME
50 minutes

EXTRAS
Flash cards (optional), a
list of sentences on
poster paper or OHP
transparency

Section B

PREPARATION
Write several commands on flash cards, for example *Put on your hat, Blow out the candle,* etc.

LEAD-IN ACTIVITIES
• You can do it
1. Get the students to stand in a circle.
2. Give a command such as: *Read a newspaper, Clean your teeth,* accompanying it with mime. Encourage everyone to imitate you. They need not speak. Choose your commands according to language and situations you have taught so far.
3. Change to giving the commands without mime and gesture.
4. Elicit the commands from the students by miming the action.
5. Ask your students to stand in two rows like this:

```
S S
S S
S S
S S
S S
 T
```

6. Say that you have commands written on flash cards. Tell the first student in each row to mime the action that they see on the flash card you show and then go to the last position in the group. Do several examples and then have a competition between teams. The first of the two front students to correctly mime a flash card command scores a point. Both go to the back of their line. Flash a new card for the two new students at the front.

• What am I going to do?
1. Write *You are going to ...* on the board.
2. Elicit sentences such as *You are going to have a cup of tea, You are going to post a letter, You are going to go to bed.* Mime what a person usually does just *before* the action you want to elicit from the students. For example, putting a tea bag into a mug and pouring hot water on it (before having a cup of tea).
3. When they are familiar with the idea, ask students to come out and do some miming in front of the class. The other learners guess what the student who is miming *is going to do.*

Variation
1. Display a list of sentences on poster paper or OHP (see the sample sentences).
2. Give your students twenty seconds or so to remember as many sentences as possible.

3. Elicit the sentences from the class by miming a prior action for each.

> *You are going to drive a car.*
> *You are going to clean your teeth.*
> *You are going to drink a cup of tea.*
> *You are going to play a guitar.*
> *You are going to pick a flower.*
> *You are going to listen to a record.*
> *You are going to paint a picture.*
> *You are going to ride a motorbike.*
> *You are going to pick some apples.*
> *You are going to ride a horse.*
> *You are going to watch TV.*
> *You are going to go for a walk in the rain.*

• **Broken promises**

1. Tell the class about one or two situations in which you had intended to do something but never did. For example:

> *You know, last Sunday I said to myself, 'I'm going to write this letter to Bill'*
> *You know what happened? The telephone rang and a friend asked me to come over to his place. So I went and didn't write the letter.*

2. Ask everyone to think of similar situations and talk about these in small groups.

PRESENTATION OF MODEL TEXT

1. Read out the model text (below) twice.
2. Ask everyone to close their eyes and imagine what the place the person lives in looks like. Read the text out again.
3. Ask several students what they have visualised. For example: Is the room big? Are there any curtains? Make sure they understand that the *I'm going to ...* sentences were said either in the morning or at the beginning of the afternoon.

Model text for young learners
'I'm going to tidy up my room
I'm going to write a letter
I'm going to help Mum
I'm going to do my homework,'
I said to myself
but then
I watched TV all afternoon.

TEXT CREATION

1. Now write the following prompts on the board and tell your students to write their own texts. Allow about five minutes.

'I'm going to _____
I'm going to _____
I'm going to _____
I'm going to _____ ,'
I said to myself
but then

_____ .

2. As students finish, they pair up or form groups and read each other their texts. If some people finish their writing much sooner than others, they can keep finding new partners.

Variation

If you work with adults you may want to use the following model text:

'I'm going to eat less
I'm going to cut down on smoking
I'm going to do more exercise
I'm going to drink less coffee,'
I said to myself
but by Friday the week had turned out
just the same as all the others.

WHEN + PRESENT

LEVEL
Intermediate +

TIME
45–50 minutes

Section A

AIM
– to highlight adverbial clauses of time (with *when*)

DISCOVERY
1. Tell the class you are going to give them a science lesson – but your science is a bit shaky! Write, or project, the following sentences on the board. Ask the students to read them and decide if they are correct or not.

When you heat ice, it expands.
When you drop glass, it bursts.
When you heat water, it melts.
When you prick a balloon, it boils.
When you set light to paper, it breaks.
When you heat metal, it burns.

2. Since the sentences are obviously *not* correct, ask the students to correct them, by re-arranging the verbs in the main clause (ie, after *it*, in each case). They can consult in pairs before giving you the answers. (If dictionaries are available, they may want to consult these).

3. The corrected sentences are:

When you heat ice, it melts.
When you drop glass, it breaks.
When you heat water, it boils.
When you prick a balloon, it bursts.
When you set light to paper, it burns.
When you heat metal, it expands.

Use these sentences to highlight the sentence structure *When X happens, Y results* to talk about general truths.

CONSOLIDATION
1. Organise the class into pairs. Copy and distribute the two versions of the gap-filled text ('Mood Swings'), so that each pair has either version A or version B (but not both!). Ask them to try and complete the poem by filling in the gaps using the words in the boxes. For those who have version A, point out that each pair of lines *rhyme*.

Mood Swings (A)

kip sigh snack bus mac fuss weep fly dip

When I'm hungry, I have a _____.
When it rains, I wear a _____.
When I'm hot, I take a _____.

When I'm tired, I have a _____.
When I'm bored, I yawn and _____.
When I'm mad, I may let _____.
When I'm late, I take a _____.
When I'm sick, I make a _____.
When I'm sad, I sit and _____.
And when I'm done, I go to sleep.

Mood Swings (B)

bored tired sad late hungry hot rains sick mad

When I'm _____, I have a snack.
When it _____, I wear a mac.
When I'm _____, I take a dip.
When I'm _____, I have a kip.
When I'm _____, I yawn and sigh.
When I'm _____, I may let fly.
When I'm _____, I take a bus.
When I'm _____, I make a fuss.
When I'm _____, I sit and weep.
And when I'm done, I go to sleep.

2. When the pairs have filled in the gaps to the best of their ability, re-group them so that each student with the A version is sitting (or standing) next to a student with the B version. They can then compare their texts.

3. Resolve any remaining doubts, eg, as to the meaning of the idiomatic expressions *have a kip* (= have a short sleep), *let fly* (= react violently), *make a fuss* (= seek a lot of attention by complaining, being restless, etc) .

4. As an optional follow-up, the poem can be recited, either by individual students, or by the class in unison.

USE

1. Write the following rubric on the board:

   What do you do, when you feel (bored/happy etc...) ?

2. Ask learners, working individually, to generate at least five questions using the rubric.

3. In pairs or small groups, they ask and answer the questions. They should make a mental note of any similarities or differences, and be prepared to report these to the class.

LEVEL
Intermediate +

TIME
50 minutes

EXTRAS
Class set of the worksheet; three strips of paper for each student

Section B

LEAD-IN ACTIVITIES
• Building vocabulary
1. Tell your students that you'll show some words for only a couple of seconds. Ask them to remember as many as possible and to note them on a sheet of paper.
2. Show words from the model text (on an OHP or a poster). When we tried out the activity with fourteen-year-olds, we used the following words:

   people   build   mountain   shout   feel
   spend   more money on   kill   fast   in a row
   cool   bombs   bored   then   world

3. After removing the word list, elicit the words. Write them on the board *exactly* as students give them.
4. Display the words again. Students check the words on the board against the list on the OHP/poster paper. Explain any words they do not understand.
5. Ask them to form meaningful sentences with the words.

PRESENTATION OF MODEL TEXT
1. Add *watching, children, than, kill* to the list above.
2. Hand out copies of the worksheet.

WORKSHEET
When it is _____
to get _____ by _____
six programmes _____,
when it is cool
to _____ cars
_____ on _____,
when it is cool
to _____ yourself on a _____ motorbike,
when it is cool
to _____ _____
that can _____ the _____ of the _____,
_____ I _____ like standing
on the highest _____
in the world and
_____ ing 'No'.

3. Ask various students to read out their solutions. Then read out the full text:
   Model text

   When it is cool
   to get bored by watching
   six programmes in a row,
   when it is cool

to spend more money on cars
than on children,
when it is cool
to kill yourself on a fast motorbike,
when it is cool
to build bombs
that can kill the people of the world,
then I feel like standing
on the highest mountain
in the world and
shouting 'No'.

TEXT CREATION

1. Ask your students to work in groups of four to six. Each student writes at least three sentences beginning with *When it is cool* on a different strip of paper.

2. Collect the strips of paper and pass them on to another group so that each group has at least twelve strips from another group. They read through them, select those which form a meaningful text and add an ending that starts with *then I feel like. ...*

3. Each group chooses a spokesperson who reads out their text.

2.8 PAST SIMPLE AND PROGRESSIVE

LEVEL
Intermediate +

TIME
40 minutes

Section A

AIM
– to introduce the past progressive in association with the past simple

DISCOVERY

1. Draw two stick figures on the board, with speech bubbles, as if in conversation with each other. The right–hand figure should have one arm in a sling.

2. Write the following jumbled dialogue on the board, or project it. Even better, write each line onto separate cards, and stick these on the board. Ask the students, working in pairs, to put the dialogue in order. Alternatively, make as many copies of the dialogue as there are pairs of students and cut up each copy into its individual lines. Shuffle these, distribute them, and ask the students to unjumble them.

I was skiing and I fell.
Yes, much better, thanks.
Did it hurt?
What's happened to you?
Are you feeling better now?
How did it happen?
I broke my arm.
You bet.

3. Check the task in open class. The most likely ordering of the dialogue is the following:

What's happened to you?
I broke my arm.
How did it happen?
I was skiing and I fell.
Did it hurt?
You bet.
Are you feeling better now?
Yes, much better, thanks.

4. Ask individual students to take one role each, and to read the dialogue aloud while the rest of the class listens.

5. Highlight the use of the past progressive and the past simple in the sentence: *I was skiing and I fell.* Point out that the past progressive provides a "frame" for the event expressed in the past simple. Elicit an alternative re-wording of this sentence using *when: I was skiing when I fell.* Or: *When I was skiing, I fell.*

6. Ask the students to invent and practise similar dialogues for these situations: a person with a broken leg, a person with a black eye, a person with a bandaged finger, a person with a bad back.

CONSOLIDATION

1. Play a variety of the game Charades where one person mimes the elements of a sentence while the others try and guess what the sentence is. First, prepare some sentences, using the structure *I was ...ing* and [past simple], for example:

   I was watching tennis and it started to rain.
   I was walking the dog and I met a friend.
   I was having a shower and the phone rang.
   I was working at my computer and the power went off.
   I was preparing dinner and I cut my finger.
   I was riding a horse and I fell off.
   I was fishing and I caught an octopus.
   I was painting the ceiling and I fell off the ladder.

   Write the sentences onto separate pieces of card or slips of paper.

2. Demonstrate the activity with one of the sentences, acting it out in sequence. Encourage the students to guess the sentence, by saying, for example, *You were playing tennis. (No) You were watching tennis. (Yes!)*

3. Whoever correctly guesses the complete sentence has the next turn. (It is important that the student says the *whole* sentence in order to claim the turn. You can use your discretion as to how exact the sentence should be. For example, you might accept *I was cooking dinner,* or *I was making dinner,* or, simply, *I was cooking,* instead of *I was preparing dinner.)*

4. Continue playing until all or most students have had a turn.

5. Ask the students, working in pairs, to write down as many of the sentences as they can remember, but using the names of the students who mimed them: *Paula was watching tennis and it started to rain.*

USE

1. Write the following *wh*-words on the board: *When...? How...? What... Who...? Where...? Why...?* Then write this pattern on the board:

   Once, when I was ...-ing, I found/lost/saw......

   Provide an example of your own, using the pattern. For example, *Once, when I was travelling in Syria, I lost my passport.* Invite learners to ask you more questions, using as many of the *wh*-words as they can.

2. Ask the students to each write two or three sentences using the pattern. Then, organise the class into groups of three, and each student takes turns to read out their sentence while the others ask *wh*-questions.

3. Invite individual students to report some of the more interesting stories to the class.

LEVEL
Intermediate +

TIME
2 lessons of
40–50 minutes each

EXTRAS
Model text copied on
OHP transparency or
44–45 index cards

Section B

PREPARATION
Copy the model text (further below) onto an OHP transparency or copy it onto index cards, one word per card.

Lesson one
LEAD-IN ACTIVITIES
• Circle clap
1. Get your class to sit in a circle.
2. Clap your hands once. The student sitting on your right has to clap hands immediately after you. Then it's the second student's turn and so on. Practise for a while in one direction until you get a smooth, rhythmical clap going round fast, then change direction.

• Associated words
1. Announce that you are going to say a word, and that instead of clapping, everyone, in turn, says a word that they associate with the word mentioned by the person before them.
2. Get your learners to do this as quickly and as rhythmically as possible. For example:

wood – squirrel – high tree – wind – ocean – across ...

• Disassociated words
Proceed as above, but this time everyone says a word they think has nothing to do with the word before. For example:

wood – salt – good – coat – really – dictionary ...

• Impromptu story: associated words
Say that you are going to tell a story. Add that anyone can interrupt you by shouting out a word which you haven't used yet but which the story brings to mind in some way. You then have to fit that word into the story. For example:

Teacher: *Once upon a time there was*
Student 1: *King*
Teacher: *Yes, a king. He had a beautiful garden*
Student2: *Witch*
Teacher: *The king had a beautiful garden that he really enjoyed, but there was one problem. At the back of the garden there was a little hut and in this hut lived a witch.*
Student3: *Midnight*

• Impromptu story: disassociated words
Proceed as above, but this time there will be more surprise elements because the students must shout out words which they think have nothing to do with the story told so far. For example:

Teacher: Once upon a time there was
Student 1:   Steam engine
Teacher: An old steam engine.
Student2:   Cow
Teacher: You will probably find it hard to believe, but this steam engine fell in love with a cow. One day
Student3:   Hot dog
Teacher: Hot dog? Yes, one day the steam engine wanted to treat the cow to lunch. The cow liked hot dogs. So they both went to a fast food restaurant.
Student 4:   Knife
Teacher: Knife, well, the cow had brought her own knife because ...

PRESENTATION OF MODEL TEXT

1. Place your transparency on the OHP with everything hidden but the first word.
2. Elicit the text word by word, each time asking students to guess the next hidden word. Use two blank sheets of stiff paper to mask then slowly reveal the text word by word: move one sheet of paper horizontally, the other one down, line by line.

   Give as little verbal help as possible, but use as many of the following types of prompt as you can:
   a. mime, gesture
   b. reveal the first letter of the next hidden word
   c. reveal words letter by letter
   d. confirm or deny the word in grammatical terms (e.g. 'No, plural', 'Use a different tense', 'Right, it is a verb').

Model text
When I got home last night
I found a toad on my bed.
It was snoring.
I was so frightened
I ran to the front door.
When I got there
It was sitting on the doorstep grinning,
'My name's John', it said
and disappeared.

Variation

If you do not have access to an OHP, try this:
1. Write words on cards, one word or word group per card.
2. Elicit the text bit by bit as above. Display the cards either by sticking them on the board or by arranging them on the floor with you all sitting around them in a circle.

Lesson two

TEXT RECONSTRUCTION

1. Cover up some words in the text (or remove some of the cards).

2. Elicit the missing words.

3. Repeat this several times, each time deleting more words.

TEXT CREATION

1. Write the following prompts on the board:

When I (the old man/my sister/friend etc.) _____
I (he/she etc.) found/realised/met/ _____
_____ was/were _____
I (he/she) _____
I (he/she) _____
When _____
_____ was/were _____
_____
_____

2. The students write their own texts, with the help of the prompts.

TEXT SHARING

Get the class into a big circle. Ask everybody, one by one, to read their text out loud.

ACKNOWLEDGEMENTS

We learnt the hand-clapping activity and the impromptu story-telling techniques from Norman Skillen. The model text is based on a text handed in to us during a workshop at Pilgrims. It is signed 'Shirley'.

2.9 MITHT

LEVEL
Intermediate +

TIME
30 minutes

Section A

AIM
– to introduce *might* to talk about possible events.

DISCOVERY
1. Draw four "frowny" faces on the board. Tell the class that they are, respectively, Sam (a surfer), Kim (a farmer), Jan (a skier), and Pat (a shepherd). Above their heads draw three thought bubbles: one showing rain, another sun, and the third snow. Check the meanings of all these words.

2. Ask the question: *Who's worried that it might rain?* (Answer: *Sam.*) *Why?* (Answer: *Because he/she wants to go surfing.*) Continue in this fashion:

   Who's worried that it might NOT rain? (Kim, because he/she wants the grass to grow.)
   Who's worried that it might snow? (Pat, because it's not good for the sheep.)
   Who's worried that it might NOT snow (Jan, because he/she wants to go skiing.)

3. Ask the students to write four sentences, one for each person, following the pattern: *X is worried that.... because ....*

CONSOLIDATION
1. On the board draw two faces with speech bubbles, as though two people were having a conversation. Underneath write the following dialogue:

   You look worried.
   I am worried.
   What's the matter?
   I'm worried I might fail my driving test.
   Don't worry about it.
   Why not?
   Nobody fails their driving test.
   I did.
   You did?
   Yes, six times.

2. Read the dialogue aloud, line by line, and ask the class to repeat it in unison. Pay attention to the correct stress.

3. Divide the class into two halves, each half representing one speaker and speaking in unison.

4. Ask two students to take each role and to read the dialogue aloud. Repeat this with other students. As each successive pair performs the dialogue, start to erase words, phrases, and eventually whole lines, so that the students are compelled to perform more and more of the dialogue from memory.

5. Finally, when there are no words at all left on the board, allow students to practise the dialogue in pairs, and then to write it out from memory.

USE

1. Prepare some sentences about possible events, either local, national, or global, each with *might,* and which each may have a negative impact on *someone.* For example,

The bus drivers might go on strike.
The price of oil might go up.
Real Madrid might not win the Champions League.
The government might ban smoking everywhere.
The mayor might lose the next election.
We might have a grammar test next week.

Dictate, write up, or project the sentences.

2. Ask the students, individually, to prepare a personal response to each sentence, of the form: *The bus drivers might go on strike, but I'm not worried because I have a bike.* They then compare their sentences in pairs or small groups, and decide who has the best reason not to be worried.

LEVEL
Intermediate +

TIME
60–80 minutes

EXTRAS
None

Section B

LEAD-IN ACTIVITIES

• A story

From memory, tell your group a story (such as the story of the boy and the coin below) in which an object gives somebody strength or exercises some curative power. Do not just read the story off the page or tell it from notes. If you want to make it as lively as possible, add details.

On his way to school, Tom had to pass a garden with a fence. Behind it there was always a big dog. Tom was worried that the dog might come out in the street one day. When one day it really did, Tom quickly crossed the street to avoid the dog and went into a shop. The old shopkeeper realised that the boy was afraid and gave him a coin. He said it would help him. When the boy left the shop, there was the dog outside. Tom put his hand in his pocket. He held the coin firmly and his fear passed. The next day he even dared to stroke the dog when it was out in the street again.

• Power objects

Elicit words for things that might have curative powers. Also elicit some information about these things, for example:

Student 1: *Picture postcard.*
Teacher: *What's the story behind it?*
Student 1: *My girlfriend sent it tome and it makes me feel good when I look at it.*
Student 2: *Fluffy animal. I always have my fluffy hamster with me when I have a test.*

As you elicit words, write them on the board.

• Changes

1. Write the following pairs of words on the board too:
afraid	*courageous*
worried	*calm*
depressed	*full of energy*
shy	*outgoing*
sullen	*lively*

2. Explain the words, giving at least one situation to clarify the meaning.
3. Ask your students to move so that there is some open space in the classroom.
4. Tell them that they are going to do an exercise in which they have to remember situations from the past, but that there won't be any talking.
5. Ask everybody to find a bit of free space to stand in.

6. Tell them to think of situations in their past which fit each one of the pairs of words on the board. Give examples:

Situation one

Some years ago I stayed in a lonely motel in Arizona. During the night I heard a couple of shots being fired. I tried to peer out into the dark night, but couldn't see anything. I couldn't get any sleep because I felt terribly afraid.

Situation two

Some months ago I was walking home from a restaurant late at night. When I turned the corner, I came upon a group of youngsters who seemed to be having an argument with an elderly man. My first reaction was to turn back, but when I realised there was something threatening about the situation, I walked straight up towards them. I was surprised how couragcous I felt. The gang disappeared and the man told me how glad he was that I had turned up.

7. Allow enough time for them to think and recall. Ask them to stand in one space on the floor for the negative situation and in another one for the positive one.

8. Tell them literally to step into the space for the negative situation and to go through it again in their mind. Give them enough time for this procedure.

9. Ask them to step out of the negative situation and literally step into the positive one by stepping into their positive space on the floor. Allow enough time for them to remember the situation again. Remind them to pay attention to any memories of colours, sounds, tastes and body movement.

10. Ask them all to choose one or more of the 'talismans' or 'power objects' listed on the board – ones which would fit into their positive recollection. Allow time for this again.

11. Ask everyone literally to step back into the negative situation again (by stepping into the corresponding floor space). But this time they should imagine taking along their chosen power object(s) and the memories of the colours, sounds and tastes from the positive situation. Ask them to reflect how their perception of the negative situation changes. It might be helpful if you list the above steps on the board.

• Sharing

If you have the feeling that your students want to share their experience, ask them to do so in pairs. Do tell them, however, that sharing means listening, but *not* judging or commenting in any way.

PRESENTATION OF MODEL TEXT

Read out the model text twice. Before reading the second time, ask everyone to imagine what the person looks like.

Model text

I was worried that I might lose my purse
I was worried that I might miss the bus
I was worried that I might forget to tell him
I was worried that he might not get any tickets
I was worried that he might not catch the train
and I was worried that he might not find me.
'Please, no more worries,' I said to myself.
And I think I've learned the trick.
When I get worried, I pick up
a magic thing and say,
'No more worries, I've had enough.'

TEXT CREATION

1. Write the following skeleton text on the board. Everyone writes a text according to the model.
2. Publication of texts.

Skeleton text

_____was worried that _____might _____
_____was worried that _____might _____

_____
_____

Variation

If you work with adults you may want to use the following model text:

He was worried
that he might not be dressed properly.
He was worried
that he might be considered stupid
when putting forward his ideas.
He was worried
that he might have laughed too much.
And he was worried
that he might have taken up
too much of his friends' time.
But on the day when he found out
that life was not a rehearsal
he packed all his worries into a bag,
walked on to a bridge
and flung them into the river.

ACKNOWLEDGEMENT
We learnt the technique for the 'changes' activity from Robert Dilts.

2.10 *WHILE* + **PAST PROGRESSIVE**

LEVEL
Lower intermediate +

TIME
40 minutes

Section A

AIM

– to introduce *while* + past progressive to talk about simultaneous past events.

DISCOVERY

1. On pieces of card or slips of paper write a number of familiar activities that can be easily and clearly performed, such as *brush your teeth, wash your face, comb your hair, put on lipstick, put your shoes on, drive a car, ride a bike, lift weights, play golf, play tennis, surf, play chess, play cards, play the guitar, play the piano, play the drums, play the violin, do the ironing, sweep the floor, wash the dishes, hang out the washing, chop wood....*

2. Distribute the cards, one per student. Ask them to keep them secret. Allow students to ask you – privately – the meaning of any words they don't understand.

3. Ask individuals to perform their actions: the others watch and guess the action. They should do this using the past progressive: *(I think) you were brushing your teeth,* etc. They can do this in open class or in groups (which may be less threatening).

4. Once you have established the names of the different activities, ask everyone to stand up and perform the activities simultaneously (you can take part too!).

5. At a given signal, everyone should stop. Get the students' attention and clearly and deliberately report on two simultaneous activities, using this model:

   While Samir was brushing his teeth, Magda was playing the violin.

   Repeat the pattern by choosing another example or two. Then invite individuals to create examples of their own, using *I: While I was washing the dishes, Ahmed was chopping wood...* etc.

6. Write some of these sentences on the board, and highlight the use of the past progressive to describe activities in progress – in this case, two activities in progress simultaneously.

7. Ask students to exchange their "action card" with another student. Everyone then repeats stages 4 and 5.

CONSOLIDATION

1. Organise the class into groups of four or five. Each person in the group should have a blank piece of paper. Tell everyone to write, on the top of the page, a sentence beginning *While* followed by the

name of a famous person, eg, *While Brad Pitt*. They then fold the top of the sheet of paper over, so that these words are hidden, and each person passes the paper to the person on their immediate right. They then each write an activity in the past progressive, eg, *was doing the dishes,* fold the paper again, and pass it on. The activity continues through the following steps:

another name (eg, *The Queen of England)*
another activity (eg, *was playing the guitar)*
the words *so they both decided to* + a conclusion.

2. They then unfold their papers and read aloud the sentences that they have jointly created. The class can then vote on the best, most bizarre, most likely, etc, scenario.

USE

1. Model the activity, by writing a sentence about yourself that describes a simultaneous activity that occurred at a specific time in the recent past, but don't mention who the other person was or what they were doing. For example,

While I was watching TV last night, someone else was doing something.
or
While I was driving home yesterday evening, someone else was doing something.

2. Ask the students to find out who the other person was by asking you yes/no questions: *Was it your husband? Was it one of your children? Was it a neighbour/friend/total stranger?* They then ask yes/no questions in order to find out what the activity was: *Was she cooking? Was she reading? Was she watching TV too?* etc, until they have guessed. Write up the full sentence, eg, *While I was watching TV last night, one of my children was doing her homework.*

3. In pairs or small groups, the students do the same.

LEVEL
Lower intermediate +

TIME
40–50 minutes

EXTRAS
OHP transparency or 14 strips of stiff paper

Section B

PREPARATION
Write the model text on transparency or on the strips of stiff paper, one line per strip.

LEAD-IN ACTIVITIES
• Mime daily routines
1. Mime various actions (having a cup of tea, reading a paper, driving a car) and ask the learners to guess what you are doing.
2. Write the words on the board or ask a student to do so. Make sure everyone gets the meaning and pronunciation of the words right.

• *like, dislike, don't mind*
1. Draw three columns on the board and draw a face on top of each – one happy, one frowning, one indifferent. Tell your students that the three faces stand for *I like, I don't like* and *I don't mind.*
2. Write the first letters of various daily routines in the columns and ask students to guess what you like, dislike or don't mind doing.
3. Encourage your learners to ask questions concerning each activity, for example:

Student 1:   *I think you don't like getting up.*
Teacher: *That's right*
Student 2:   *You don't like to shave.*
Teacher: *That's also true. I don't like shaving.*
Student3:   *Why don't you like it?*
Teacher: *Well, sometimes I cut myself, it takes time, I have to do it again the next morning.*

• Guessing game
1. Form pairs.
2. Each student writes down two activities they think their partner likes / dislikes / doesn't mind doing.
3. They read out their speculations and their partners confirm or deny them. Ideally, students should work with partners they do not know well. Time permitting, they may change partners several times.

• Mental images
1. Tell your students that you are going to say a stem sentence which you want them to finish in writing.
2. Give an example: *While I was coming to school... "Let's say you were thinking about the homework you didn't do, so you write down 'I was thinking about the homework I didn't do'."*
When you have said a stem sentence, ask everyone to close their eyes and to wait for a clear mental image of what they had been doing. Only when they have this image do they complete the stem

For example:

Teacher: *While I was washing up I was thinking of...*
Student 1: *A large garden.*
Student 2: *A letter I wanted to write.*

PRESENTATION OF MODEL TEXT

1. Show your students the first line of the model text very briefly (OHP or flash cards). Tell them to write it down. Use the same technique with each line.
2. Ask everyone to compare their text with a partner.
3. Ask several students, one by one, to read out their texts.
4. Display the whole text. Read it out as well, in order to give your students a model of pronunciation and intonation.

Model text
While I was having breakfast
I was thinking about my boss.
While I was crawling along in heavy traffic
I was thinking about the pile of work
waiting for me.
While I was at work
I was thinking about a peaceful evening
in front of the TV,
and while I was watching TV
I was thinking about how difficult it is
to fall asleep.
I am always
ahead of my time.

TEXT CREATION

Write the skeleton text on the board. Ask your students to write their own texts. They may change the last two sentences if they want.

Skeleton text
While I (he/she) was _____
_____
While _____
_____
While _____
_____
and while _____
_____
I am (he/she is)
always ahead of my (his/her) time.

2.11 THIRD PERSON *-S, DOESN'T*

LEVEL
Elementary

TIME
40 minutes

Section A

AIM
- to introduce the third person form of the present simple, affirmative and negative

DISCOVERY
1. Collect four to six objects that you might find in a person's possession, such as in their handbag or briefcase, and which are evidence of their habits and interests. The objects shouldn't bear the person's name. They could be a bus pass, a concert ticket, the photo of a cat or dog, the card of a Japanese restaurant, a bar of chocolate, etc.

2. Tell the class that you found these items in a bag on the school premises, and that you are trying to identify the owner. Check that the students know the names of the different items, and ask individual students and/or the whole class to repeat them.

3. Hand out the objects, so that the students can examine them closely. Ask the class whether they think the person is male or female, young or old.

4. Then elicit sentences based on what they can tell, from the objects, about the person's lifestyle. For example:

    He (or she) takes the bus every day.
    He (or she) likes classical music.
    He (or she) eats Japanese food.
    He (or she) likes chocolate.
    He (or she) likes animals.
    etc.

5. Write the sentences on the board as they are elicited. When all the sentences are written up, ask individual students to read them aloud.

6. Erase the verbs from the sentences, and see if the students can remember them

7. Ask individual students questions based on these sentences. For example: *Do YOU take the bus everyday? Do YOU like classical music?* etc. If any students answer negatively, say, *So, it's not YOUR bag.*

8. Write examples of negative sentences, using the appropriate students' names, alongside the affirmative ones that are already on the board. For example.

He (or she) likes classical music. But Ana doesn't like classical music.
He (or she) eats Japanese food. But Ernesto doesn't eat Japanese food.

Highlight the form of the verb (*likes, doesn't like*) in each case.

CONSOLIDATION

1. Organise the class into a circle, either seated or standing. Start a memory "round", by saying your name and something that you like, using this formula: *My name's Scott, and I like olives.*

2. Point to the first student to your left, and explain that they must repeat your sentence, but in the third person (*His name's Scott and he likes olives*) and add a statement about themselves (*My name's Paolo and I like cheese...*). The next person continues in this fashion, repeating the previous statements and adding their own (*His name's Scott and he likes olives. His name's Paolo and he likes cheese. My name's Sandra and I like tomatoes.*) This continues until all the students have had a turn.

USE

1. Ask the students, working individually, to write six true sentences about themselves on a slip of paper, three beginning *I like...* and three beginning *I don't like...*

2. Collect the slips, shuffle them, take one out at random and read out the six sentences that are written on it. Ask the other students if they can guess who wrote them. Whoever wrote the sentences can then confirm the correctness (or not) of the guess. Continue like this until all, or most of, the sentences have been read out.

LEVEL
Elementary

TIME
30 minutes

EXTRAS
(Optional) OHP

Section B

PREPARATION
If you have a OHP, write the model text on a transparency.

PRESENTATION OF MODEL TEXT
1. Present the text below on an OHP transparency or on the board.
2. Read the text out.
3. Tell your students to close their eyes. Ask them to imagine what the girl looks like. Read the text a second time.
4. Ask them a couple of questions about her looks.

Model text
She likes animals
she likes flowers
she likes good stories
but
she doesn't like
one thing:
lies.

TEXT RECONSTRUCTION
1. Put a mask on the transparency (or erase words from the board) so that your students can only see the following:
   She _____
   she _____
   she _____
   but
   she _____
   _____ :
   _____

2. Ask them to say the original version.

TEXT CREATION
1. Tell your learners to close their eyes and think of a person they want to write about.
2. Ask them to create their own texts based on the above prompts. Have your students read their texts out loud. They may, of course, use he instead of *she.*

Here are two texts written by ten-year-old beginners.

She likes English	*She likes beautiful flowers*
she likes French	*she likes her dolls*
she likes biology	*she likes* boys
but	*but*
she doesn't like	*she doesn't like*
one thing:	*two things:*
unfair teachers.	*thieves and school.*

2.12 PAST TENSE FOR NARRATIVE

LEVEL
Lower intermediate +

TIME
40–65

Section A

AIM
– to review past simple (for narration) and past simple questions

DISCOVERY

1. Place two chairs opposite each other at the front of the class. Invite one student from the class to take the "hot seat". Sit in the other chair yourself.

2. Ask the student six to ten questions about the events of a defined time in the past, eg, last night, the last weekend, or a recent holiday. Typical questions might be: *What did you do on Saturday? Where did you go? Who did you go with? Did you have fun? What did you do then?* etc.

3. Once the interview stage is over, the student returns to his or her seat. Then, elicit from the class the main events that the student reported, and write these on the right-hand side of the board, in the first person. Eg, *On Saturday I went to the cinema. I went with two friends. We saw ….* etc

4. Next, ask the class if they can remember the questions that you asked to get this information. Write up one or two example questions: *Where did you go? Who did you go with?* Ask the class, working in pairs, to reconstruct the rest of the questions.

5. Write all the questions on to the board. Draw attention to the form of the past tense in both the answers and the questions: *I went → Did you go?*

CONSOLIDATION

1. Set the scene by reporting a recent event in your life, such as *Last month I went to Portugal,* or *Last weekend I went to a party.* Tell the class that they are going to write a short account of that event, and so they need to ask you questions. But instead of *speaking,* they are going to ask the questions in *writing*.

2. Organise the class into about three or four groups. Distribute a dozen or so slips of blank paper to each group. (It helps if each group has different coloured paper.) Among themselves each group decides on a question they want to ask, in order to get information that will be useful for their report. They write the question on one of the slips of paper and one member of the group delivers the question to you. If the question is correctly formed (and relevant), write the answer on the same slip of paper. The "postman" then returns to the group where the answer is read and a new question formulated and delivered to you for answering. If a question is not well formed, send it back, perhaps with some indication as to what the problem is.

3. When each group has assembled sufficient information about the event, they can then start to use this information to write an account of the event (which should be in the third person). Monitor this stage and suggest any changes or corrections. During this stage the groups are allowed to "post" you more questions if they find that they are lacking important information.

4. When the accounts have been written, each group passes their text to the group on their right. The texts are read, and then passed on to the next group. Because the questions that each group asked will be different, each group's text will also be different. These differences make an interesting focus for an open class discussion stage at the end. For example, ask individuals to mention any differences they found between the text that their group wrote, and the texts that other groups wrote.

USE

1. Write a "headline" that summarises – and exaggerates – a recent event in your life, for example: *Shopping Disaster*. Or *Weekend Traffic Horror*. Or *Tennis Triumph*. Invite the class to ask you questions to get the gist of the story.

2. Students now do the same: they write on a piece of paper their own headline in large, legible script.

3. Half the class stand around the room holding their headlines so that these headlines are clearly visible. The other half (the "interviewers") each position themselves opposite one of the students who is holding a headline, and ask them questions about it. After a minute or so, call out "Change!", and the interviewers move clockwise so as to face the next "headline", and begin asking questions again.

4. Once all the interviewers have interacted with all the "headlines", the roles are reversed: those who were doing the interviewing now stand with their own headlines and are themselves interviewed.

5. Some of the most interesting stories can then be reported back to the whole class.

LEVEL
Lower intermediate +

TIME
40–50 minutes

EXTRAS
A class set of the model text

Section B
PRESENTATION OF MODEL TEXT
1. Form groups of three or four.
2. Assign a letter (A, B, C, D) to each student in each group.
3. Give everyone a copy of the model text.
4. Ask groups to read the text and make up a background story for it. You may want to give them a few guiding questions for their work.

Model text
This morning I saw a woman
on the bus to school.
Her face was swollen
and her eyes were filled with tears.
Did she notice that everybody was
staring at her?
Did she see the two kids
laughing at her behind her back?
Did she hope that somebody would
ask her about her sorrow or
did she want to be left alone?
I did not try to talk to her either.
Do not ask me why.

Guiding questions
What do you think had happened to the woman before she got on the bus?
How many people were involved in the incident?
How did each of these behave?
What do you think was the motive for their behaviour?
What do you think happened after the woman got off the bus?

• Story-telling
1. Form four new groups by putting all the As, Bs, Cs and Ds together.
2. Ask everyone to tell the other group members their background story.

• Finding a similar situation
1. The narrator of the incident described above was not quite sure of what was going on. Ask your students to identify with the narrator and speculate about his or her feelings in the situation. Ask them if they would have reacted likewise or totally differently.
2. Allow several minutes for everyone to recall a situation where they had feelings similar to those of the narrator.
3. Ask them to express in the form of a mind map what they remember about this situation (eg, below).

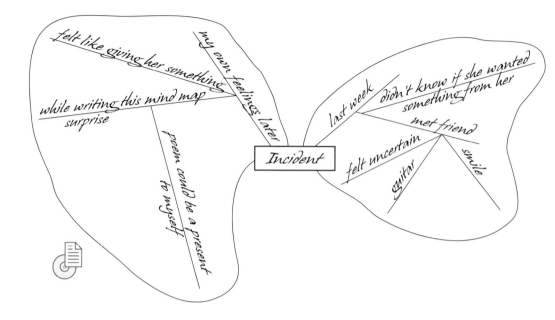

TEXT CREATION

1. Point out or elicit the following about the model text:
a. opening statement (lines 1 and 2)–general
b. focus on person (lines 3–4)–specific
c. four reflective questions (lines 5–11)
d. narrator's behaviour (line 12)
e. addressing the reader (line 13)
2. Ask your students to write their own texts based on this non-linguistic structure.

This example is by the student who produced the mind map above.

Last week I met a friend of mine,
a guitar in her hand,
her eyes a little sad,
her lips trying to smile,
her hand reaching out for something.
Did she notice I was there?
Did she want me to talk to her?
Did she really want me to do something
for her?
I wrote a poem for her.
I could have written it to myself.

Elisabeth Schweiger

2.13 PRESENT PERFECT (HAVE YOU EVER ...?)

LEVEL
Lower intermediate

TIME
40 minutes

Section A

AIM
– to reinforce the use of the present perfect with *ever*.

DISCOVERY
1. Write this sentence on the board:

   I have seen a flying saucer.

2. Check the students' understanding of the sentence by asking concept checking questions. For example:

   Do we know when this happened? (Answer: *No*)
   Did it happen some time in my life? (Answer: *Yes*)

3. Elicit ways of making the sentence negative. For example:

   I haven't seen a flying saucer.
   I have never seen a flying saucer.

4. Establish the meaning of *never,* ie, 'not once in my entire life'.

5. Elicit the question form, ie,

   Have you ever seen a flying saucer?

   Establish that *ever* means: 'in your entire life'.

6. Elicit other words or phrases that could substitute for *flying saucer,* and write them on the board so as to form a table:

Have you ever seen	a flying saucer? a shooting star? a space ship? the rings of Saturn? a total eclipse? etc.

7. Draw attention to the form of the present perfect, ie, *have* + past participle.

CONSOLIDATION
1. Elicit the verbs associated with the five senses, ie *see, hear, taste, smell*, and *touch.*

2. Organise the class into small groups. Ask each group to produce at least one question of the type *Have you ever...?*, using each of these verbs. For example, *Have you ever seen a ghost? Have you ever heard a wolf?*

3. Ask the students to stand up and circulate, asking and answering their questions, and noting the answers. To do this, they will need pen and paper, and a book to support their writing on.

4. When all or most of the students have interacted with each other, ask them to return to their original groups to collate the results of their survey. This should take the form of sentences of the type: *Two people have seen a ghost. No one has heard a wolf,* etc.

5. Ask a spokesperson from each group to report some of the more interesting facts they have discovered.

USE
1. Write the following table on the board:

One of us Two of us Three of us All of us None of us	*has* *have*	*been to* *seen* *met* *eaten* *had* etc.	....

2. Organise the class into groups of four. The task of each group is to generate as many true sentences – using the above table – as possible. You can set a time limit, eg, five minutes. Or you can make it a race, eg, the first group to generate 12 sentences is the winner. To generate the sentences, learners will need to ask one another questions using *Have you ever....?*

3. Ask individuals to report on some of the more interesting sentences that their group produced.

LEVEL
Lower intermediate

TIME
20–30 minutes

EXTRAS
(Optional) flash cards;
OHP necessary for the
variation

Section B

PREPARATION
(Optional) write infinitives of irregular verbs on flash cards, one per card.

LEAD-IN ACTIVITY
• Back writing
1. Tell your class to get together in threes and decide who is A, B, and C.
2. Ask the As in each group to look at you, the Bs and Cs to turn their backs to you. Nobody is allowed to talk. Mime an action (one expressable by an irregular verb) or show it on a flash card. The As now turn around and write the past form of this verb on the Bs' backs with their fingers. The Bs write the past participle of the verb on the Cs' backs. The Cs, in turn, note down the infinitive of the verb on a piece of paper and put it face down on a desk. Demonstrate the activity first with three students in front of the class. Then continue with ten to twenty words.
3. Read out the list of verbs you started with and ask each group to check how many of the verbs they got right.

PRESENTATION OF MODEL TEXT
1. Present the skeleton text and ask your learners to complete it in pairs (each dash stands for one letter):

Skeleton text
Ha _ _ yo _ ev _ _ , ev _ _ , ev _ _
i _ yo _ _ li _ _
ri _ _ _ _ a cr _ _ _ _ _ _ _ ?
N _ , I ha _ _ ne _ _ _ , ne _ _ _ , ne _ _ _
ri _ _ _ _ a cr _ _ _ _ _ _ _ ,
b _ _ I on _ _
ro _ _ a dr _ _ _ _ .

2. Ask a few learners, one by one, to read out their texts. Then read out the original:

Model text
Have you ever, ever, ever
in your life
ridden a crocodile?
No, I have never, never, never
ridden a crocodile,
but I once
rode a dragon.

TEXT CREATION

Students write their own texts based on the model.
The following texts were written by twelve-year-olds in their second year of English.

Have you ever, ever, ever
in your life
swum in tomato soup?
No, I have never, never, never
swum in tomato soup,
but I once
found a fly in my tomato soup.

Have you ever, ever, ever
in your life
shouted at your teacher?
No, I have never, never, never
shouted at my teacher,
but she once
shouted at me.

Variation

1. Show a range of irregular verbs on flashcards and tell your learners to mime the verbs.
2. Now using the same cards, elicit the past form of each verb and ask the students to say sentences using the past starting with *Once. ...* Proceed like this for a few minutes to give your learners sufficient practice of the structure before you go on to the next stage.
3. Display the following 12 sentences on the OHP, read them out and clarify the meaning of words your learners don't know.

Have you ever eaten an earthworm?
Have you ever written a love poem?
Have you ever lost your schoolbag?
Have you ever drunk cod-liver oil?
Have you ever told a lie?
Have you ever found some money?
Have you ever caught a bat?
Have you ever seen a ghost?
Have you ever broken a window?
Have you ever bought some junk?
Have you ever ridden a camel?
Have you ever been to London?

4. Students study the list for a minute and then you switch off the OHP.
5. Ask them each to say the sentence they like best.
6. Present the model text about riding a crocodile (above), then ask your students to write their own texts.

If you work with adults you may want to use the following model text:

Have you ever, ever, ever
in your life
made another person look like a perfect idiot?
No, I've never, never, never
made another person look like a perfect idiot,
but I once
made a complete fool of myself.

2.14 PRESENT SIMPLE

LEVEL
Lower intermediate +

TIME
40 minutes

Section A

AIMS
– to review present simple statements, both affirmative and negative
– to introduce defining relative clauses

DISCOVERY

1. Write – or project – the following unfinished definitions on the board, and ask the students to try to complete them:

> A *film buff* is a person who...
> A *football fan* is a person who ....
> An *animal-lover* is a person who ...
> A *bookworm* is a person who....
> A *shop-aholic* is a person who...
> A *vegetarian* is a person who....

2. Write up the students' suggestions, making them more accurate if necessary. For example:

> A *film buff* is a person who likes films.
> A *football fan* is a person who loves football.
> An *animal-lover* is a person who likes animals.
> A *bookworm* is a person who reads a lot.
> A *shop-aholic* is a person who shops a lot.
> A *vegetarian* is a person who doesn't eat meat.

3. Highlight the form of the definition, including the use of the defining relative clause (beginning with *who)* and the use of the present simple.

4. Erase (or mask) the terms for the people (*film buff, football fan* etc) and see if students can remember them.

CONSOLIDATION

1. Write the following questions on the board:

> Are you a *real* film buff?
> Are you a *real* football fan?
> Are you a *real* animal-lover?
> Are you a *real* shop-aholic?

2. Tell the students that they are going to work in groups to design some survey questions in order to answer one of the above questions. The questions should take the form of *Are you the sort of person who....?* For example, *Are you the sort of person who has seen* Casablanca *ten times?*

3. Organise students into groups of four. Assign one category of person to each group (ie, *film buff, football fan, animal lover, shop- aholic).* Give each member of the group a letter of the alphabet: A, B, C, D. The students work together to prepare at least four or five questions.

4. Re-group the students by asking all the As in the class to sit together, all the Bs to sit together, and so on. The students then ask one another their questions, noting the answers. Each student then decides who in the group is the most/least like the type of person in question.

5. Ask individual students to report some of their more interesting findings to the class.

USE

1. Ask students to draw the outline of their two hands on a piece of paper. Tell them that the left hand represents "the people they like" and that the right hand represents "the people they don't like". On each finger of the left hand, therefore, they should write an adjective that completes the sentence *I like people who are....* For example, *I like people who are funny.* On each of the fingers of the right hand they should write a negative adjective, eg, *mean.* Allow students to use dictionaries, if available.

2. In pairs, students compare their "hands", looking for similarities and differences.

3. You can display these hands (labelled with the names of their owners) around the walls of the classroom. Younger learners might like to decorate them.

LEVEL
Lower intermediate +

TIME
At least 80–100 minutes (or a series of 2 or 3 45–minutes lessons)

EXTRAS
A ball of string or wool; photos; one large sheet of poster paper for each student; cassette of soft, meditative music

Section B

PREPARATION
Before class, ask students to bring along a photo of themselves.

LEAD-IN ACTIVITIES
• Opening up a field of awareness
1. Show your class a photo of someone you like.
2. Tell them a few things about this person, for example, how you got to know him/her, a story about him/her, etc.
3. Ask your students to work in groups and write a list of this person's positive qualities. They should include positive qualities that they think this person has, not only the things you have told them about.
4. Ask your students what they have written and list what they say on the board, for example:

He/She	*likes to laugh.*
	helps you when you have a problem.
	cares about doing things right.
	hardly ever gets angry.

5. Ask the students to think of people they like, and ask them to add positive qualities to the list you have started.

• *I like you because*
1. Arrange your class in a circle sitting down.
2. Throw your ball of string to one student and tell this person what you like about them. For example, 'Peter, I like you because you are a good listener'.
3. Ask Peter to wind the string around his finger and throw the ball to another person in the group addressing them in the same way (eg, 'Karen, I like you because you are friendly.')
4. Allow seven to ten minutes for the game. Then go back to the list you have started and, with the help of your students, add a few more positive qualities.

Note
The preceding activity can noticably enhance positive feelings that already exist among participants. Less obvious, perhaps, is the potential of an activity like this for alerting you to any participants who are isolated from the rest of the class. A teacher experienced in facilitating group dynamics can use the insights gained to integrate the student(s) into the group. (See especially Stanford 1977.)

• Positive self presentation
1. Ask your students to think of qualities other people like about them. Tell them that various people like different things about each of us. What their parents like about them might be totally different from what their best friend at school or their favourite teacher likes. Perhaps add a few examples about yourself.

2. Ask your students to stick their photographs in the middle of a big sheet of poster paper and to write around the photo the positive qualities they think others see in them.
3. When they have finished, get them to close their eyes and imagine themselves five years on from now.
4. Play some soft, meditative music. You can help your students with the visualisation of their positive future self by guiding them, as follows.

Find a comfortable sitting position ... with your back straight and your feet firmly on the ground... and for a while focus on the contact you have with your chair... and the floor below you ... and while you are listening to the sound of the music ... and the sound of my voice ... you can also direct your attention to other noises you can hear at the moment... the noise of the cars passing by ... and the footsteps of the people walking along the corridor past our classroom (substitute whatever sounds you can really hear in your class for these) *... and now you can listen to your own breath ... as you breathe in and breathe out... in a natural rhythm ... in and out. and while you are sitting there in your chair ... listening to my words ... imagine yourself five years on from now ... imagine that you are actually travelling into the year X ... on a day like today ... you are now five years older... you can feel that you have grown ... and developed in a very positive way ... you have made things possible for yourself that you were dreaming would come true five years ago ... just feel what it is like to have all these positive qualities that you now have ... and how other people react to you as you have changed ... and how you enjoy this ... take some time now to experience this new feeling . . . while you're listening to the sound of the music* (allow two minutes) *... you feel very light and happy and now you slowly start walking back through the years to the here and now. Take your time, all the time you need and slowly, slowly come back to the here and now. Slowly open your eyes and stretch a little, welcome back to your classroom.*

5. Ask your students to add their 'future' positive qualities to their posters. Tell them to use the same language structure as above so that they actually present themselves as having these qualities already.

PRESENTATION OF MODEL TEXT
1. Write the first two words of the model text on the board.
2. Elicit the text from the learners word by word, giving them as little verbal help as possible.
3. As you elicit the text, write it in the vertical layout shown below. (If you do not have freckles, you might want to adapt the text slightly so that it fits you personally.)

Model text
I
don't
like

people
who are too noisy,
who talk all the time,
who tell lies,
who laugh about my freckles.
I
like
people
who are friendly,
who can listen
and who are honest.

RECONSTRUCTION OF MODEL TEXT
1. Tell your students that you want them to study the model text carefully.
2. Give them a minute.
3. Then cover the text up.
4. Elicit the text word by word, starting at the last word and working backwards. Write the text on the board as you go along.

TEXT CREATION
1. Ask everyone to write their own text based on the model. The following skeleton text might be helpful:

Skeleton text
I don't like people
who _____
who _____
who _____
I like people
who _____
who _____
and who _____

2. Students stick their texts on the poster they have created. Display the posters on the walls around your classroom.

Variation
If you work with adults you may want to use the following model text:

I don't like people
who can't listen
who never read books
who smoke when I'm still eating
and who gossip about others.
I like people
who are energetic
who love children
who fight against stupidity
and who care about the fate of our planet.

CHAPTER 3
QUESTION FORMS

3.1 QUESTIONS

LEVEL
Lower intermediate +

TIME
45 minutes

Section A

AIM
– to raise awareness about basic question formation

DISCOVERY

1. Prepare sets of cards, one set per group of three or four students. Write a selection of short questions on the cards, one word or phrase per card. Use capital letters, so that there are no punctuation clues as to the word order. For the same reason, on separate, smaller cards, prepare as many question marks as there are questions.

For example, here is a set of four four-phrase questions, suitable for a lower intermediate group:

WHERE	WERE	YOU	BORN	?
WHAT	ARE	YOUR	HOBBIES	?
HOW LONG	HAVE	YOU	LIVED HERE	?
WHO	DO	YOU	LOOK LIKE	?

2. Organise the class into small groups and hand out the sets of cards, one per group. Tell the students to sort the cards into questions, indicating the number of questions that there are and the number of cards that make up each question. Ideally, the students should be able to spread out the cards on a flat surface.

3. When most of the groups seem to have finished, elicit the correct combinations and write them on the board.

4. Use these examples to highlight the following features of questions:

   a. inversion of (auxiliary) verb and subject (*Where were you born? What are your hobbies?*)
   b. use of "dummy" auxiliary *do* where there is no auxiliary verb already (*Who do you look like?*)

5. In pairs, students can ask each other, and answer, the questions.

CONSOLIDATION

1. Copy and hand out – or project – the following matching task.

a. *What do you do?*	*No, I live with my parents.*
b. *Are you married?*	*Six months now.*
c. *Do you have your own flat?*	*No, I'm single.*
d. *Are you seeing anyone?*	*He's a student.*
e. *How long have you been together?*	*I sometimes sing in a group.*
f. *What does he do?*	*I'm an assistant in a bookshop.*
g. *How do you spend your free time?*	*Heavy metal.*
h. *What kind of music do you like?*	*Yes, I have a boyfriend.*

2. Ask students, working individually and then comparing in pairs, to match the questions with the answers.

3. When you have checked the task, mask the questions, or ask the students to fold their papers in half so that the questions are hidden. In pairs they then try and reconstruct them, using the answers as clues.

USE

1. Using the above questions – or similar – students interview one another in pairs. Then they write a short summary of the information they have found out.

2. Monitor the writing stage to ensure that the summaries are more or less correct. Then collect them and display them around the room. If possible, ask students to supply photos to go with each "interview".

LEVEL
Lower intermediate +

TIME
60–80 minutes

EXTRAS
None

Section B

LEAD-IN ACTIVITIES
• Find the questions

1. Write a few words on the board. They should be related to you personally to make the activity motivating for your students, for example:
    17 years
    Queen Charlotte Islands
    red
    Yes, I am.
2. Tell your students that these words are answers to personal questions about you that they are supposed to ask you. To avoid lengthy spans of silence help with the questions by using mime.
3. Whenever they successfully elicit one of the answers on the board from you, tick the word(s) concerned. The actual questions to the answers above are:

    How long have you been a teacher?
    Where are you going for your next holiday?
    What colour is your car?
    Are you married?

    Note, however, that in order to make this activity motivating for your students it is essential that the words you have written on the board are related to you personally.

• Interview your teacher

1. Tell your students to imagine that they are doing a personal interview with you. Tell them you will answer any question they ask. Give them time to think of at least three questions.
2. Ask them to write their questions down.
3. Then tell them the following:

Close your eyes and imagine you are asking me your questions one after another. Imagine what answers I am going to give you. Take your time. When you think you know what I'm going to answer, open your eyes again and note down what you think my answers would be.

4. Put your students into pairs or groups. Tell them to share their questions and the expected answers.
5. Ask your class to sit in a semi-circle with you at the front. Tell them that you are now really going to answer their questions as openly as you can. Say that, although highly unlikely, it could happen that you feel you do not want to answer one of their questions. And if so, you will say the question is too personal.
6. After your students have finished their interviews ask them to compare the answers you gave with the ones they expected. This can be done as a class activity or in small groups. It can trigger off both intensive discussion in class as well as give you a very good insight into how your students perceive you.

Variation

Immediately after you have responded to the question, ask your students to compare each answer with the answer they expected.

PRESENTATION OF MODEL TEXT

1. Write the following gapped text on the board:

When _____ _____ _____ _____ _____ _____ ?
Why _____ _____ _____ _____ ?
Why _____ _____ _____ _____ _____ _____ ?
– three questions I _____ .
Can _____ _____ _____ _____ _____ _____ ?
Do _____ _____ _____ _____ _____ _____ _____ ?
What's _____ _____ _____ ?
– three questions I _____ .

2. Ask the class to guess the missing words. Whenever somebody comes up with a correct guess, write it in. We have seen teachers use mime, gesture, nodding, and silent mouthing of words to elicit whole texts from their students without themselves saying a single word. A more direct form of prompting is to give the first letter of a word and get your learners to guess.
This is the text you should end up with on the board:

Model text
When are you going to do this?
Why didn't you come earlier?
Why didn't you think before you spoke?
– three questions I hate.

Can I talk to you about this?
Do you think what I did is okay?
What's your favourite song?
– three questions I like.

• Speculation about the model text

1. Organise your students into pairs. Get them to imagine as many details as they can about the person who wrote the text above. Give them a few questions to guide them, for example:

How old do you think the person is?
What does he/she look like?
What are his/her interests?
Do you think this person would be interesting to talk to? Give your reasons.
The person mentions six questions in the text. Who do you think asked these questions?

Have all the questions been asked by the same person?
Select one of the questions mentioned in
the text. Describe what you think actually happened.

2. Ask each pair to report their findings.

RECONSTRUCTION OF MODEL TEXT
1. Ask your students to look at the model on the board for a short period of time.
2. Then, while they are still studying the text, quickly rub most of it out leaving only the following:

_____ ?
_____ ?
_____ ?
– _____ *questions I* _____ .
_____ ?
_____ ?
_____ ?
– _____ *questions I* _____ .

3. After twenty seconds ask students to reconstruct the text orally.

TEXT CREATION
Then get them to write a text based on the model. Tell them that they can include any number of questions they want.

TEXT SHARING
Tell your students to stand up, mill around and find a partner. The students read their texts to each other. A lively talk among the pairs might follow. When a pair have finished, they each find another partner to read their texts to.

Variation
If you work with adults you may want to use the following model text:

Why didn't you tell me beforehand?
What's the point of all that?
How come *you haven't finished?*
– three questions I hate.
How was your day?
Would you like to join us?
What other choices have we got?
– three questions I like.

3.2 *WHAT IS* + ADJECTIVE?

LEVEL
Elementary–lower
intermediate

TIME
30 minutes

Section A

AIM
– to teach questions formed by *what is* + adjective

DISCOVERY
1. Dictate or write up the following question:

   What's grey and has four legs and a trunk?

   If necessary, allow students time to consult with each other or use a dictionary. If students answer *An elephant,* answer, *No, it's a mouse going on holiday.* You will probably need to explain the play on words, ie, *trunk* = elephant's nose AND a large suitcase.

2. Now, repeat the procedure with this question:

   What's brown and has four legs and a trunk?

   (Answer: A mouse coming back from a holiday)

3. Use the two questions to highlight the use of *what* as the subject of the question.

CONSOLIDATION
1. Copy and hand out this matching exercise. Explain that the questions and answers are all elephant jokes. (If you are teaching adults you may want to point out that these are children's jokes, so are not necessarily very funny!) Students can work in pairs, using dictionaries if available.

1. *What's big and grey and wears a mask?*
2. *What's grey with red spots?*
3. *What's yellow on the outside and grey on the inside?*
4. *What's grey and never needs ironing?*
5. *What's grey and goes round and round?*
6. *What's big and grey and has 16 wheels?*
7. *What's grey but turns red?*
8. *What's big and grey and protects you from the rain?*

a. *An elephant with the measles!*
b. *A drip dry elephant!*
c. *An elephant in a washing machine!*
d. *An elephant on roller skates!*
e. *The elephantom of the opera!*
f. *An embarrassed elephant!*
g. *An umbrellaphant!*
h. *An elephant disguised as a banana!*

2. Check the answers, and explain the jokes if necessary. (The answers are: 1 – e; 2 – a; 3 – h; 4 – b; 5 – c; 6 – d; 7 – f; 8 – g.) Ask the students which joke (if any!) they found the funniest.

USE

1. Challenge the students to design their own jokes, using the formula *What's X and has/does etc Y?* Students can work in pairs or groups of three. Remind the students that the jokes don't have to be very funny. Nor do they have to be about elephants – they could also be about mice, frogs, or crocodiles, for example.

2. Ask volunteers from each group to ask one of their jokes to the rest of the class.

3. Vote on the best (or worst!) joke.

LEVEL
Elementary–lower
intermediate

TIME
30–40 minutes

EXTRAS
None

Section B

PRESENTATION OF MODEL TEXT
• Read out the model text.

Model text
What's hard? Tests on Monday.
What's short? Games on Sunday.
What's frightening? An angry teacher.
What's fun? Ice cream after school.

• **Gathering associations**
1. Go to the board and write the word *school*.
2. Ask your learners to shout words to you. Add all these words onto the board.
3. Form pairs and ask each to group the words on the board under the following headings: *frightening, interesting, difficult, okay, hard, long, relaxing, unfair, great, fun, short.*
4. When they have finished, ask each pair to add words from other topic areas (not school) under each of the headings.
5. Ask each pair to read their words out.

TEXT CREATION
1. Ask everyone to lay out their word lists in the centre of the classroom. The spread of papers becomes a word source for writing in step 3.
2. Read out the model text once or twice more.
3. The students write their own texts based on the model. Encourage them to stroll around the centre of the room checking the word lists from time to time.

Variation
If you work with adults you may want to use the following model text:

What's hard?
Getting up on Monday mornings.
What's fun?
Watching men ironing.
What's great?
A glass of wine after a hard day's work.
What's relaxing?
Lying in a hot bath.
What's off-putting?
Someone picking their nose.

3.3 QUESTIONS WITH *DO*

LEVEL
Elementary

TIME
45 minutes

Section A

AIMS
– to review the different uses of *do/does*
– to focus on question formation with *do/does*

DISCOVERY

1. Copy and distribute – or project – the following film titles.

   1. **Do** You Love Me?
   2. Boys **Do**n't Cry
   3. Alice **Does**n't Live Here Anymore
   4. **Do**n't Look Now
   5. Where **Do** We Go from Here?
   6. **Does** This Mean We're Married?
   7. Please **Do**n't Eat the Daisies
   8. They Shoot Horses, **Do**n't They?
   9. What Did You **Do** in the War, Daddy?
   10. Why **Do** Fools Fall in Love?

2. Ask the students, working in pairs, to identify and classify the different uses of *do/don't, does/doesn't*. If you think the class needs some guidance, you can provide them with the following grid which they can fill in with examples from the titles:

auxiliary verb		main verb
question	negative	

3. Check the task. Here is how the grid should be filled in:

auxiliary verb		main verb
question	negative	
1, 5, 6, 8, 10	2, 3, 4, 7, 8	9

Note that (8) is both negative and a question. You could further subdivide the uses of the auxiliaries according to the number and person, or whether they are imperative. For example:

	singular	plural
first person		5
second person	1	
third person	3, 6	2, 8, 10

imperative	4, 7

4. Copy and hand out (or project) the following worksheet, and ask the students to complete it from memory.

   1. _____ *You Love Me?*
   2. *Boys _____ Cry*
   3. *Alice _____ Live Here Anymore*
   4. _____ *Look Now*
   5. *Where _____ We Go from Here?*
   6. _____ *This Mean We're Married?*
   7. *Please _____ Eat the Daisies*
   8. *They Shoot Horses, _____ They?*
   9. *What Did You _____ in the War, Daddy?*
  10. *Why _____ Fools Fall in Love?*

CONSOLIDATION

1. Write the following table on the board:

1	2	3	4
Why	do	fools	fall in love?

2. Elicit other words or phrases that can go into column 3 of the table. Do the same with column 4.

3. Have a race. In pairs or small groups, ask students to generate as many questions as they can by changing elements in columns 3 and 4. The pair or group that can produce the most questions in one minute are the winners.

4. Ask individuals to read out some of their questions, and see if anyone can answer them!

USE

1. Read, or project, the following information about some of the films mentioned in the *Discovery* phase:

Don't Look Now is a thriller. It was filmed in Venice in 1973. It stars Donald Sutherland and Julie Christie.

Boys Don't Cry is a drama, made in 1999 starring Hilary Swank. It's based on the true story of a boy who is really a woman.

Please Don't Eat the Daisies is a comedy starring Doris Day. It was made in 1960.

Why Do Fools Fall in Love (1998) is a bio-pic, based on the life of a 50s pop singer who died tragically young.

Where Do We Go from Here? is a musical starring Fred MacMurray and it was made in 1945.

2. Draw attention to the *types* of film that are mentioned: *thriller, drama, comedy, bio-pic* (ie, a picture based on someone's biography), and *musical.* Elicit other types of films, eg, *horror, science fiction, costume drama, western, animation,* etc.

3. Ask individual students *Do you like thrillers/musicals* etc? *What's your favourite comedy/ horror film* etc?

4. Ask the students, working in pairs or small groups, to compose similar questions in order to find out each other's taste in films. When they have four or five questions, ask them to stand up and circulate, asking and answering their questions. They should remember any opinions that match their own, and report these to the class at the end of the activity, using this formula (which you can write on the board):

X likes horror films, and so do I.
Y doesn't like costume dramas, and neither do I.

LEVEL
Elementary

TIME
40 minutes

EXTRAS
A soft ball or a knotted scarf; model text on OHP transparency or poster paper

Section B

LEAD-IN ACTIVITIES

• The teacher's likes and dislikes

1. Ask your students to write down three things that they think you like and three they think you do not like. Tell them that they should not include anything that everybody knows about you, but speculate about things that are not commonly known about you.
2. After a minute ask everyone to pair up and pool their notes.
3. Pairs join up into groups of four and produce joint lists.
4. One member of each group reads out their speculations to the class. You record the guesses on the board in two columns.
5. Comment on the guesses and ask questions, for example:

Why do you think I don't like pop music?
It's true that I like cooking. Do any of you like it too?

• The learners' likes and dislikes

1. Get the class into a circle.
2. Toss your ball to someone and address them like this:

Suzanne, do you like animal films?

If Suzanne answers with yes, go on asking until her answer is no.
3. Then it is her turn to throw the ball to another member of the group. Continue in this way for about three minutes.

PRESENTATION OF MODEL TEXT

1. Tell the class that you are going to present a text to them (on OHP) and read it out to them. Tell them they'll have ten seconds to study the text after you finish reading it. Say you'll remove the text and they'll have to write down what they can remember.
2. Read out the text below.

RECONSTRUCTION OF MODEL TEXT

1. In pairs, students try to rewrite the whole text.
2. When they have finished, ask someone to come to the board. The class dictate and this student writes the text on the board.
3. Display the original model text for comparison.

She asked,
'Do you like sport?'
I said no.
She asked,
'Do you read a lot?'
I said no.
She asked,
'Do you like rock music?'
I said no.

She asked,
'What do you like?'
I said,
'Raindrops on the window.'

TEXT CREATION

1. Everyone writes two lists about themselves under these headings:

Things lots of people know I don't like
Things not many people know I don't like

2. Students write their own texts based on the model and the prompts below. Allow about five minutes.

He / she asked,
_____
_____

He / she asked,
_____
_____

He /she asked,
_____
_____

He / she asked,
_____
_____

I said,
_____

3. Presentation of texts.

3.4 QUESTIONS IN THE THIRD PERSON ...

LEVEL
Lower intermediate

TIME
45 minutes

Section A

AIMS
– to review adverbs of frequency
– to review question forms with *why do...?*

DISCOVERY

1. Draw the following cline (ie, graded line) on the board, and ask students to copy it:

100%

0%

2. Dictate the following adverbs of frequency and ask students, working individually, to place them on the cline in the appropriate place. Demonstrate what you mean by writing *always* at the top end of the cline.

never
sometimes
rarely
often
almost always
almost never

3. Ask students to check in pairs, and then hand the board pen to one student and ask them to write *never* on the cline in the appropriate place. Continue with the other adverbs. Note that *sometimes* has a much wider range than the other adverbs, and can extend from almost zero to over 50%.

CONSOLIDATION

1. Dictate – or write on the board – the following sentences:

Boys cry.
Chickens fly.
Politicians lie.

Dogs smell.
Babies yell.
Teenagers rebel.

Girls chatter.
Old people get fatter.
Exams matter.

2. Ask the students, working individually, to choose an adverb of frequency for each sentence and place it in the correct position in the sentence. For example:
Boys almost never cry.
Old people often get fatter.

3. Organise the students into pairs or groups of three and ask them to compare their answers. Encourage them to come to an agreement on an adverb in each case: this may mean that they will have to persuade one another.

4. Elicit one example from one of the groups. Eg, *Boys almost never cry.* Turn into a question, with *Why*: *Why do boys almost never cry?* Write this on the board, and elicit some possible answers.

5. Ask the students to turn the rest of their statements into *why–* questions and to write these down.

6. They should then all stand and circulate, asking their questions and taking note of some of the better answers. They can then report these to the whole class.

USE

1. Write the following table on the board:

Why do	some people parents teachers children adults boys girls etc.	always never sometimes rarely often almost always almost never	....?

2. Ask students, individually, to think of a question, using this model, that they would really like answered. For example, *Why do some people always jump the queue? Why do boys often fight?* They should write their question at the top of a blank sheet of paper.

3. Each student then passes their question to the person sitting on their right. They each read the question they have been given, and write an answer *on the bottom of the paper.* They then fold the answer over, so that it is out of sight, and hand the paper on to the next person, who does likewise. This continues until the paper returns to its original owner, who then opens out the answers, reads them, and selects the best one. These can then be read out to the whole class.

LEVEL
Lower intermediate

TIME
30 minutes

EXTRAS
One large sheet of poster paper for each group of four to five students; (optional) dictionaries

Section B

LEAD-IN ACTIVITIES

• Noun search

1. Ask your learners to work in groups of four.
2. Hand out one large sheet of poster paper to each group.
3. Ask everyone to note down on their sheets of paper as many nouns as they can think of. Countable nouns should be put in the plural, however. Give some examples. If they use dictionaries, encourage them to go beyond what they have been taught so far.

• Sentence creation

1. Working in pairs, students create sentences based on the following structure:

Why	does	...	always	taste of	...
	do		often	smell of	
			sometimes	sound like	
			rarely	look like	
			never	feel like	

Ask your students to create as many combinations as possible and to include unusual ones such as *Why does popcorn always smell of hamsters?*

2. Elicit their sentences and write them onto a sheet of poster paper.
3. Display the poster on the wall so that everybody can see it easily.

TEXT CREATION

1. Ask your class to form new pairs or groups.
2. Ask each group to create a text by selecting some of the sentences from the poster paper and arranging them so that they read like a poem. They may want to give their text a title. Here is an example written in one of the classes in which this technique was tried out:

Why does popcorn always smell of hamsters?
Why does work often taste of tea bags?
Why does poetry sometimes sound like rain?
Why does the lunch break rarely look like roses?
And why does war never sound like music?

3. The students then read out their texts in class.

ACKNOWLEDGEMENT

This lesson has been adapted from an idea in *The Inward Ear* (Maley and Duff 1989, p.138).

3.5 *WHICH* AS INTERROGATIVE PRONOUN

LEVEL
Intermediate + (adults)

TIME
45 minutes

Section A

AIMS
– to introduce *which* as an interrogative pronoun
– to review comparative forms of adjectives

DISCOVERY
1. Copy – or project – the following picture of sharks.

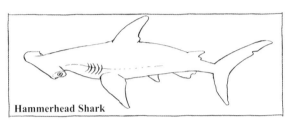

Hammerhead Shark

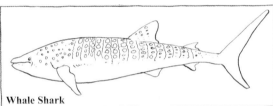

Whale Shark

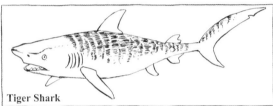

Tiger Shark

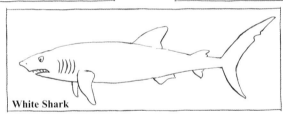

White Shark

2. Dictate – or write up – the following questions:

Which is bigger – the Whale Shark or the White Shark?
Which is longer – the Tiger Shark or the Hammerhead Shark?
Which is more aggressive – the Tiger Shark or the White Shark?
Which is more dangerous – the Whale Shark or the Tiger Shark?

3. Ask students to discuss these questions in pairs and suggest answers. They should use this model (which you can write on the board):

We think that the X shark is bigger/ more aggressive/ more dangerous than the Y shark.

4. Copy and hand out the following text, which the students should read silently, in order to see if they were correct or not.

The **Tiger Shark** weighs up to a tonne, and is about five metres long. It is extremely aggressive. It likes shallow water. So it's very dangerous to swimmers.
The **Whale Shark** grows up to 15 metres long and weighs up to 20 tonnes. Despite its large size it is harmless to people.

The **White Shark** is the strongest and most aggressive of all sharks. It can grow up to 6 metres long and weigh 3 tonnes. It prefers the open sea, but it will occasionally attack swimmers.

The **Hammerhead Shark** lives in tropical waters. It weighs around half a tonne and averages around three metres in length. It has an aggressive character and can be quite dangerous.

5. Check the answers. Ask students which of their initial answers were correct/incorrect.

6. Go back to the original questions and highlight the form *which is* + comparative adjective?

CONSOLIDATION
1. Draw two large concentric circles on the board. Elicit the names of some animal pairs and write these in the outer circle. You can prompt ideas by giving one "half" of a pair. For example: *dog/cat; tiger/lion; African elephant/Indian elephant; gorilla/chimpanzee; polar bear/brown bear; eagle/falcon; blue whale/sperm whale; cobra/python*, etc.

2. Elicit adjectives that could be used to describe animals and write these in the inner circle. For example, *small, large, strong, dangerous, intelligent, fast, deadly, friendly, common, rare*, etc.

3. Elicit a question using *Which....?* that uses words on the board. For example, *Which is stronger: the gorilla or the chimpanzee?*

4. Answer the question using a "frame" such as the following, and write it on the board:

I'm not sure, but I think the gorilla is stronger.
I'm pretty sure that...

5. In open class, the students then each take turns to formulate a question based on the words on the board. They should nominate who they wish to answer it.

6. Those questions that they can't answer – but are keen to answer – can be set as the basis for a homework task: Try and find the answers in an encyclopedia or on the internet!

USE

1. Write up a pair of popular brand names – for trainers, for example, or for cars, or for mobile phones. Pose the question: *Which is better: X or Y?* Respond to students' answers by asking *Why do you think so?*

2. Ask the students to prepare and conduct a "market survey" of the rest of the class. To do this, they first work in groups of three or four to prepare some questions, using *Which is* + comparative. Give each member of the group a letter: A, B, C, D. When they have prepared five or six questions, re-group the students by asking all the As in the class to sit together, all the Bs to sit together, and so on.

3. Each student asks the questions they have prepared, taking notes of the answers. Remind them to ask *Why?* questions, as well as *Which?* questions.

4. The students then return to their original group to collate their answers, and to prepare to report on them to the whole class. To provide a guideline for this, write the following rubric on the board:

   [number] *out of* [number] *people in the class think that X is better than Y. This is because ..... and .....*

LEVEL
Intermediate + (adults)

TIME
40 minutes

EXTRAS
Class set of gapped text B; OHP and transparency

Section B

PREPARATION
Write the following words on an OHP transparency:

is lacking	*belong*	*depend on*	*integrity*
realise	*valuable*	*fulfilment*	*fame*
rejoice	*destructive*	*failure*	

LEAD-IN ACTIVITY
• Remember the words
1. Tell your students that they will have only a few moments to look at the words. They will have to remember them and are not allowed to write anything down.
2. Switch off the OHP. Ask your students to write down as many words as they remember.
3. They then call out the words. You write them on the board.
4. Add the ones they may not have remembered. Ask them to form meaningful sentences with the words.

PRESENTATION OF MODEL TEXT A
1. Read out model text A to your class.
2. Ask students to close their eyes. Read the text again, slowly.
3. Say that you are going to read out the text a third time. Ask everyone to note down – while you are reading – any associations they have with the text (eg, what they disagree with, people or situations they are reminded of, etc.). If necessary, give an example.
4. Then discuss the content of the text. Ask also what associations they had.

Model text A
Fame or integrity: which is more important?
Money or happiness: which is more valuable?
Success or failure: which is more destructive?
If you look to others for fulfilment, you will never truly be fulfilled.
If your happiness depends on money, you will never be happy with yourself.
Be content with what you have;
rejoice in the way things are.
When you realise there is nothing lacking,
the whole world belongs to you.
Lao Tse, Tao Te Ching (chapter 44)

In one of the trial classes the students seemed to agree with everything the text says. The teacher got a discussion going by giving a few personal examples:

The text says 'Be content with what you have'. This makes me think of a situation in my life when I really wanted to have a new car. I really wanted to have it. So I finally bought it. Once I had it, it was not at all important for me any more.

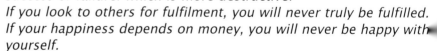

PRESENTATION OF MODEL TEXT B
1. Hand out copies of gapped text B.
2. Tell your students that each dash stands for a letter. Ask them to fill in the blanks individually and then check with their partner(s).

Gapped text B
Wo _ _ _ o _ act _ _ _ _ : wh _ _ _ a _ _ mo _ _
effe _ _ _ _ _ ?
Lo _ _ _ o _ char _ _ _ _ : wh _ _ _ i _ mo _ _
convi _ _ _ _ _ ?
Know _ _ _ _ _ o_ curi _ _ _ _ _ : wh _ _ _ i _ mo _ _
valu _ _ _ _ ?
It'_ n _ _ wo _ _ _ th _ _ co _ _ _ ,
it'_ act _ _ _ _ ,
it' _ n _ _ lo _ _ _ th _ _ co _ _ _ ,
it'_ char _ _ _ _ ,
it' _ n _ _ know _ _ _ _ _ th _ _ cou _ _ _ ,
it'_ curi _ _ _ _ _ .

3. Read out the model text for the final check:

Model text B
Words or actions: which are more
effective?
Looks or charisma: which is more
convincing?
Knowledge or curiosity: which is more
valuable?
It's not words that count,
it's actions,
it's not looks that count,
it's charisma,
it's not knowledge that counts,
it's curiosity.

TEXT CREATION
Ask your students to work in pairs and to write their own texts. They can then read them out or display them in the classroom.

Note
You might want to tell your students that the *Tao Te Ching by* Lao Tse is an ancient Chinese book of wisdom. Stephen Mitchell's inspiring translation (1988) also contains an excellent introduction.

3.6 WHO DOES IT BELONG TO?

LEVEL
Lower intermediate +

TIME
30 minutes

Section A

AIM
– to teach questions and answers with the verb *belong*

DISCOVERY

1. Make a show of collecting five or six personal items from individual students in the class, such as a ring, a mobile phone, a pen, a watch, a dictionary, a personal stereo. Check that the class know the names of these items in English. For fun, also have a large denomination note (such as fifty euros) accessible but hidden.

2. Hold up the objects one by one, and ask *Who does this belong to?* and *Does this belong to you?* Write the questions on the board. When the ownership of an item is identified, say *It belongs to X,* and write this on the board as well.

3. Finally, produce the fifty euro note and ask *Who does this belong to?* When individual students (jokingly!) claim the note, say *No, it doesn't belong to you. It belongs to me!*

4. Highlight the questions and answers on the board, eliciting a translation (if the class is monolingual) or a paraphrase (if they are not), such as *Whose is this?* (for *Who does this belong to?*).

5. Ask one student to come out, to take the role of the teacher, with a new set of objects borrowed from the class.

CONSOLIDATION

1. Prepare a set of true and false statements, with *belong*. For example:

   a) *The South Pole belongs to Australia.*
   b) *The Beatles songs belong to Michael Jackson.*
   c) *Michelangelo's David belongs to the Vatican.*
   d) *Tahiti belongs to France.*
   e) *The USA once belonged to Britain.*
   f) *China belongs to Hong Kong.*
   g) *Part of the Moon belongs to the USA.*
   h) *Buckingham Palace belongs to the British Royal Family.*

You can also include some local information, such as any landmark that belongs to a private individual, a university, and so on.

2. Copy and distribute the sentences and ask students to rate them true or false, working in pairs or small groups. Those that they believe are false they should try and correct.

3. Check the task in open class. The answers for the sentences above are:

1. *false:* the South Pole belongs to nobody.
2. *true:* at least, he owns the publishing rights to most Beatles songs.
3. *false:* in fact, the ownership of this statue is contested between the Italian government and the city of Florence.
4. *true.*
5. *true.*
6. *false:* Hong Kong belongs to (The People's Republic of) China.
7. *false:* none of the Moon belongs to anybody (although bits of moon rock belong to various people and organizations).
8. *false:* it belongs to the British nation

USE

1. Play a guessing game, using objects that clearly belong either to the people in the room, or to the school or institution. Demonstrate this by saying *I'm thinking of an object in this room. Can you guess what it is?* Insist that students ask only *yes/no* questions, including *Does it belong to...?*

2. Students take turns sitting at the front of the class and being "it", ie, the person thinking of the mystery object. Whoever guesses the object correctly takes a turn as "it". If students are forgetting to ask questions with *belong,* you can make it a rule that, for each turn, at least one *belong* question must be asked, before the person who is "it" yields their turn.

LEVEL
Lower intermediate +

TIME
30–40 minutes

EXTRAS
Cassette of soft, meditative music; several sheets of poster paper, felt–tip pens; class set of model text

Section B

LEAD-IN ACTIVITIES
• Visualisation

1. Play some soft, meditative music. Ask your students to seat themselves comfortably with their backs straight and their bodies in a relaxed position.
2. Lead them into a guided visualisation. For example:

Feel your contact with your chair and the floor ... allow yourself to relax while you are listening to my voice and the sound of the music ... and if you want to ... you can come with me now... and imagine that you are now standing in the middle of a beautiful meadow... feeling the warmth of the sun on your skin ... and the gentle breeze ... and when you look down you can see the soft, green grass and the flowers... and you start to walk, feeling the grass under your feet... take your time and do everything at your own pace ... and while you are walking along ... looking around you ... seeing all the beautiful colours of the flowers around you ... and the butterflies and the birds ... you can feel a sense of freshness and joy
... take all the time you need to feel the grass and to look around as you walk and then, slowly, at your own pace you return to our classroom ... take your time ... slowly open your eyes ... take a deep breath and stretch a little, welcome back.

• Creation of posters

1. Switch off the cassette recorder. Put several sheets of poster paper and a box of felt–tip pens of different colours on the floor.
2. Ask your students to jot clown whatever comes to mind (words, sentences, pictures). Play some soft music again while they are doing this.

• Reflection

1. Stick all the posters on the wall.
2. Get your students to sit in front of the posters in a semi-circle.
3. Let students comment on the posters, ask each other questions or talk about their experiences during the guided visualisation.

PRESENTATION OF MODEL TEXT

1. Give each student a photocopy of the model text below (or show it on the OHP, write it on the board or read it out).

Who does it belong to,
the blue of the sky
on a beautiful morning in September?
Who does it belong to,
the singing of the birds
in the trees by the river?
Who does it belong to,
the smile on your face
when we happen to meet among the crowd?

2. Ask your students to study the text for two minutes.
3. Get them to remember the text without looking at it.
4. Elicit the text and write it on the board.

TEXT CREATION
1. Clear the text off the board.
2. Ask students to work in pairs and write their own texts following the pattern below, which you can dictate or write on the board.
3. Ask them to think of a title for their text.

Who does it (do they) belong to,

___ ___

___ ___ ___ ___ ___ ___ ___ ___

___ ___ ?

Who ___ ___ ___ _

___ ___ ___

___ ___ ___ ?

Who ___

___ ___

___ ___ ___ ?

CHAPTER 4
COMPLEX SENTENCES

4.1 *IF* + PRESENT PROGRESSIVE

LEVEL
Intermediate +

TIME
30 minutes

Section A

AIMS
- to highlight the use of *always* + present progressive to talk about annoying habits
- to introduce the sentence pattern: *if* + present progressive (for giving advice)

DISCOVERY
1. Write the following dialogue on the board, and read it aloud:

    A: *My dog barks all the time.*
    B: *That's nothing. My dog is always barking!*

2. Ask the students to say why B's statement sounds more forceful, more emphatic. The answer is that the use of the present progressive "stretches" the activity, making it sound non-stop and continuous. Point out that, because of this, the present progressive + *always* is often used to express annoying habits. For example, *My brother and sister are always fighting.*

3. Continue the dialogue by writing a third line:

    A: *If your dog is always barking, take it to the vet.*

Point out that this use of an *if*-clause plus an imperative is a way of giving advice.

4. Ask the students to work in pairs and to write similar, three-line, dialogues that begin with the following lines:

    My teeth hurt.
    My teacher shouts at me.
    My Dad smokes a lot.

5. Ask pairs of students to read their dialogues aloud, taking different roles.

CONSOLIDATION
1. Copy and hand out the following exercise. Ask students to match the two halves of each sentence. They can do this individually and then check together in pairs. Allow them to consult dictionaries, if available:

If your neighbours are always having parties	tie it up.
If your phone is always ringing	hide them.
If your dog is always running away	eat something.
If your nose is always running	feed them.
If your sister is always borrowing your things	go and join them.
If your stomach is always rumbling	ignore them.
If your friends are always making fun of you	unplug it.
If your cats are always miaowing	blow it.

2. When you have checked this task, ask the students to mask the left-hand column, and, working in pairs, to try and reconstruct the *if*-clauses.

USE

1. Write on the board *Someone is always reading my emails.* Elicit some possible ways of dealing with this problem, beginning *If someone is always reading your emails….* For example, *…change your password; …lock your computer; … send yourself an email, saying that someone is reading your emails!*

2. Ask students, individually, to think of a problem they have experienced because of someone else's annoying habits. Distribute some blank cards, about the size of a playing card, so that everyone has one. On one side they should write their problem, in the form of a sentence beginning *Someone is always…*

3. Collect the cards, and re-distribute them. If anyone receives their original card, take it back and give it to someone different. Ask everyone to read the problem and then write, on the back of the card a suggestion, in the form of a sentence beginning *If someone is always….* Make sure they leave space for at least two other responses.

4. Collect the cards, and repeat the last stage. Do this one more time until each card has three pieces of advice. Collect the cards, and take one at random. Read out the problem, and then the three pieces of advice. Ask the class what advice was best. Do the same with a few more of the cards.

LEVEL
Intermediate +

TIME
50 minutes

EXTRAS
OHP transparency of poem 'Mart's advice'; (optional) class set of jumbled text B and gapped text C

Section B

PRESENTATION OF MODEL TEXT A

1. Display text A on the OHP. Explain any words that you think your students won't be able to guess.
2. Read the poem out twice. The students work in groups of three.
3. Turn off the OHP. Two members of each group try to reconstruct the text in writing from memory. Call up the third member of each group. Show them the text and give them two minutes to study it before returning to their groups.
4. The third student then assists the other two members in reconstructing the text.

Model text A
Mart's advice:

If someone's acting big with you,
if someone's bossing you about,
look very hard at one of their ears.
Keep your eyes fixed on it.
Don't let up.
Stare at it as if it was
a mouldy apple.
Keep staring.
Don't blink.
After a bit
you'll see their hand
go creeping up to touch it.
They're saying to themselves
'What's wrong with my ear?'

At that moment
you know you've won.

Smile.

McGough and Rosen, *You Tell Me – there's no Ale in it.* Puffin Books 1981, p.31

• Checking the text

1. Several groups read out what they have written.
2. Read out the original version again.
3. Present text A on OHP or poster paper again so that the students can correct their texts.

PRESENTATION OF MODEL TEXT B

1. Hand out a copy of jumbled text B or write it on the board and ask the students to unscramble it.
2. They read their versions out. Then you read out the original.

Jumbled text B
take out a mirror,
'What's this all about?'
or 'Einstein', 'Karl Marx' or
'the Marx Brothers.'
if someone's laughing at you,
Keep holding it
Smile, pocket your mirror and then
put your hand in your pocket,
If someone's teasing you,
After a while they'll ask
hold it to their face.
so that you feel very small,
slowly say, 'Freud'
if someone's pulling your leg,

Model text B
If someone's teasing you,
if someone's pulling your leg,
if someone's laughing at you,
so that you feel very small,
put your hand in your pocket
take out a mirror,
hold it to their face.
Keep holding it.
After a while they'll ask
'What's this all about?'
Smile, pocket your mirror and then
slowly say, 'Freud'
or 'Einstein', 'Karl Marx' or
'the Marx Brothers.'

TEXT CREATION

1. Ask everyone to write down at least two sentences starting with *don't like people who....* Ask some students to read out their sentences. For example:
   I don't like people who never listen.
   I don't like people who complain all the time.
2. On the board write a sentence called out by a student.
3. Show your class how to transform this sentence so that it fits the structure of the model text. For example:

   I don't like people who never listen
   becomes
   If somebody never listens to you

   I don't like people who never look at me
   when I say something
   becomes
   If someone never looks at me when I say something

4. Get your learners to transform ten to fifteen sentences in this way

   If somebody always interrupts you
   If somebody never cares for your feelings
   If somebody never shows any gratitude
   If somebody tells you lies
   If somebody talks about you behind your back

5. The students write their own texts individually or in pairs. Ask some of them to read their texts to the class or to each other in groups.

4.2 WHENEVER

LEVEL
Lower intermediate +

TIME
30 minutes

Section A

AIM
– to introduce the use of time clauses with *whenever*

DISCOVERY

1. Write or dictate the sentence *Every time I see a shooting star, I make a wish.* Check that students understand *shooting star* and *make a wish.*

2. Ask students to think of one word that could replace *every time.* If they can't think of it, teach them *whenever.* Erase *Every time* and substitute *Whenever…*

3. Elicit other sentences of a similar type, by asking, for example, *What do you do whenever you see a black cat? What do you say whenever someone sneezes?*

CONSOLIDATION

1. Distribute, or project, the following poem, and ask students to fill in the gaps using words in the box. They can work individually at first, and then compare their answers in pairs.

blue	depressed	bright	best	alright

Whenever I'm with you
I feel ____.
Whenever I'm with you
The future's ____.

Whenever you're not here
I'm really ____.
Whenever you're not here
I miss you.

Whenever we're apart
I'm _____.
But whenever we're together
It's the _____!

2. Check the task (the missing words are – in order – *alright, bright, blue, depressed, best.*

3. Say each line of the poem, and ask the class to repeat it, paying attention to the rhythm.

4. Ask the students, in pairs, to practise saying the poem. Then call on volunteers to recite it to the class.

USE

1. Ask the learners, working in pairs, to write at least one more verse of the poem. It's not important that it rhymes, so as long as the sentiment is right. To help, here are some possible first lines:

   Whenever you're away...
   Whenever I'm by your side...
   Whenever I hold your hand...

2. Students can then exchange and read each other's verses.

LEVEL
ower intermediate +

IME
0 minutes

XTRAS
one

Section B

PRESENTATION OF MODEL TEXT

1. Write *whenever* on the board.
2. Tell the students that it is the beginning of a sentence you have in mind. Ask them to shout words to you. Help them to guess what follows by using mime and gesture. Whenever a student gives you a correct word, note it onto the board as below.

Whenever
my teacher
looks at
me
through
his
thick
glasses
I
feel
very small.

Variation

If a student offers a word you aren't looking for, write it to one side and try to use it to build up a new vertical text which incorporates it. Sometimes you can end up with several texts as shown below. This array was created in one of our trial classes with thirteen–year–olds at the beginning of their third year.

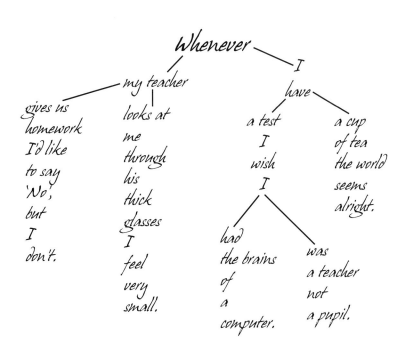

TEXT INTERPRETATION
1. Get your students to read through the model text again.
2. Ask them to say why the writer feels small. Note their suggestion on the board. This is what a class of thirteen–year–olds came u with:

The writer
– never does his homework
– is new at school
– plays truant
– steals
– doesn't like the teacher
– is always nervous
– is bad at school
– cheats a lot
– plays lots of tricks on his teacher

3. Ask them to speculate what they think the reasons for the person' behaviour could be. Note these speculations on the board too. Her are the suggestions from the above class:

The writer
– comes from a broken home
– has lots of problems with his parents
– is often hit by his parents
– 's mother is dead. His father has no time.
– is stupid
– takes drugs
– watches too much TV
– is a bit crazy

TEXT CREATION
Ask your students to create their own texts based on the model text The following texts were written by learners from the trial class:

Whenever
my dog
eats his
food with
his big
teeth,
I feel
good
because
he doesn't
need any
food for
the rest of
the day.

Whenever
my football team
has lost
a match
our trainer
feels angry,
and
so
do
I.

4.2 WHENEVER

Variation
If you work with adults you may want to use the following model text:

Whenever
my colleagues at work
say a cheerful 'Good morning',
I ask myself
how those people always manage
to get out of bed
on the right side.

ACKNOWLEDGEMENT
We owe the idea for the model text *(Whenever my teacher...)* to the late Hans–Eberhard Piepho.

4.3 *IF–* SENTENCES + PAST PERFEC[T]

LEVEL
Intermediate +

TIME
40 minutes

Section A

AIM
– to introduce the third conditional (*if* + past perfect)

DISCOVERY

1. Write *Lucky? Or Unlucky?* at the top of the board, and draw tw[o] neutral faces underneath. Tell the students that they are about [to] hear two stories, and they have to decide if the person in each sto[ry] was lucky or unlucky.

2. Point to the first face and read (or tell) the following:

   This is Sam. He had a plane to catch. But on the way to the airpo[rt] his taxi broke down and he was late arriving so he missed t[he] flight. That particular flight crashed and everyone was killed.

3. Ask *Was Sam lucky or unlucky?* If there is some doubt, tell the sto[ry] again. Establish that Sam was lucky and challenge the students [to] tell you why. It is likely that someone will try to produce a senten[ce] with *If...* Help them formulate this, and write it on the board, in th[e] form: *If he had caught the plane, he would have been killed.* Or: [If] *he hadn't missed the plane, he would have been killed.*

4. Point to the second face and read this text:

   This is Cindy. Every week she buys a lottery ticket with the sam[e] number: 2222. Last week she didn't have the right change, so sh[e] didn't buy a ticket. You guessed it. Last week the winning numbe[r] was 2222 and the prize was nearly a million dollars.

5. Repeat the procedure above (stage 3), this time establishin[g] Cindy's bad luck, and eliciting, and writing up, the sentence: *If sh[e] had bought a ticket, she would have won nearly a million dollars.*

6. Highlight the form and the meaning of the two sentences (abou[t] Sam and Cindy). Establish the "hypothetical past" meaning, eg, b[y] asking *Did Sam catch the plane?* (Answer: *No*). *Did Cindy buy [a] ticket?* (Answer: *No*). *Can they change things?* (Answer: *No*). Poin[t] out the use of the past perfect in the *if*–clause, and the use c[of] *would* + the perfect infinitive in the main clause. You could als[o] point out the typical contractions that occur in spoken language, i[e]

   If he'd caught the plane, he would've been killed.
   If she'd bought a ticket, she would've won nearly a million dollar[s.]

7. Elicit further sentences about each situation, by asking, fo[r] example, *What would have happened if Sam's taxi hadn't broke[n] down? What would have happened if Cindy had had the rig[ht]*

change? Write the answers on the board, eg, *If Sam's taxi hadn't broken down, he wouldn't have been late. If Cindy had had the right change, she would've bought a ticket.*

8. Progressively erase each sentence from the board, removing a word at a time, while asking individual students to repeat the sentence, until no words are left.

9. In pairs, students should then try to reconstruct all the sentences by writing them down from memory. As an optional extra, they could also write their own versions of the short texts about Sam and Cindy.

CONSOLIDATION

1. Copy and distribute – or project – the following jumbled sentences.

   a. *she/got wet/If/wouldn't/had/have/taken her umbrella/Claudia*
   b. *scored a goal/lost/Ben/we/If/would/lost the match/hadn't/have*
   c. *Tibor/passed the exam/he/studied harder/If/would/had/ have*
   d. *saved her document/Monica/she/have/If/wouldn't/lost it/had*
   e. *chased the cat/If/wouldn't/the dog/hadn't/have/it/been run over*
   f. *Tommy/slept in/had/he/If/wouldn't/set his alarm clock/have*

2. Ask the students, working in pairs, to unjumble them.

3. Still in pairs, the students should then write a mini–situation (like the Sam and Cindy stories) that leads up to each of these six sentences. (Alternatively, assign one mini–situation to different pairs.)

USE

1. Tell the class a true story about yourself or someone close to you, where you were either lucky or unlucky, and where events could have taken a different course. But, just before the end of the story, withhold the conclusion. For example,

   Once, when I was travelling in the Middle East, I was sitting in an outdoor café, having a cup of coffee. Next to the café some workmen were doing some work on a building. For some reason, I decided to move to another table. Five minutes later, a huge wooden beam slipped from the grasp of one of the workmen, and fell onto the seat where I had been sitting...

2. Challenge the class to provide an *if*–sentence to complete the story. Eg, *If you hadn't moved, you would've been injured or even killed!*

3. Ask the students to do the same: first to compose, then tell to their neighbour, a story whose conclusion would be an *if*–sentence. Their neighbour has to supply the missing *if*–sentence.

4. Ask individual students to tell their neighbour's story to the class.

LEVEL
Intermediate +

TIME
50 minutes

EXTRAS
(Optional) Class set of
worksheet

Section B

LEAD-IN ACTIVITIES
• Questions that change the story
1. Write the following on the board:

What would have happened if ...	*hadn't...*	*kissed (Sleeping Beauty?)*
	had ...	*(kissed the queen instead of Sleeping Beauty?)*

Announce that you are going to tell a fairy tale, a folk tale or a story. Ask your class to interrupt you whenever they want to.

2. Tell your story, pausing frequently to encourage students to interject past conditional questions. If students do not interrupt you, prompt them somehow (eg, by gesture). As students ask questions, answer them and adapt the story accordingly. For example:

Student: *What would have happened if Little Red Riding-Hood had looked through the window before entering her gran's house?*
Teacher: *She would have known that it wasn't her gran lying in bed. So she would have run back the way she had come, clutching her basket.*
Student: *What would have happened if the wolf had realised that she was running away?*
Teacher: *He would have stormed out of the house to try to catch Little Red Riding-Hood. So let's say he was running after the little girl who, however, after a while, happened to look back. When she saw the wolf, she froze...*

• Tell your own story
1. Form groups of four. Each group member should tell a story. The other three in the group must each ask two questions with which they can change the course of the story.
2. Each student finds a partner from another group and tells both their own original story and the story that resulted due to the questions asked in the group phase.

PRESENTATION OF MODEL TEXT
1. Hand out the following worksheet (or write both texts as well as the words in the box on the board).
2. Ask everyone to complete the sentences by filling in the gaps with words from the box underneath.

Worksheet

If she had _____ me	*If I had _____ her roses*
I would have _____ .	*she would have _____ me*
If she had _____ at me	*and if she had _____ me*

I would have _____
_____ for her.
If she had _____ me to
I would have _____ a song.
If she had _____
I would have _____ a poem
and if she had _____ me
I would have said 'Yes.'

I would have _____ her cheek
and if I had _____ her cheek
she would have _____
and if she had _____
I would have _____ her
That her cheeks were
the colour of roses.

> kissed – blushed – embraced
> – looked at – told – bought –
> blushed – asked – written
> – embraced – smiled – kissed –
> nodded – painted a picture
> – blushed – composed – wanted –

3. Ask your students to read out their texts.
4. Present the model texts.

Model texts

If she had looked at me
I would have blushed.
If she had nodded at me
I would have painted
a picture for her.
If she had wanted me to
I would have composed a song.
If she had smiled
I would have written a poem
and if she had asked me
I would have said 'Yes.'

If I had bought her roses
she would have embraced me
and if she had embraced me
I would have kissed her cheek
and if I had kissed her cheek
she would have blushed
and if she had blushed
I would have told her
that her cheeks were
the colour of roses.

TEXT CREATION
The students write their own texts based on the model. Follow up with presentations of these texts to the whole class.

4.4 REPORTED SPEECH

LEVEL
Intermediate +

TIME
40 minutes

Section A

AIM
– to highlight the features of reported speech

DISCOVERY

1. Copy and hand out – or project – the following jumbled dialogue. Alternatively, copy the dialogue and cut it up into its individual lines. Give each group a set of lines so that they can physically unjumble them.

She:	I'm too busy to talk.
She:	You don't talk, you whine!
She:	Jack was talking to *me*.
She:	No, I'm not. Why?
He:	I'm also talking to you!
He:	You won't talk to me.
He:	You don't seem to be too busy to talk to Jack.
He:	Are you mad at me?

2. Check the task. The most likely order is the following:

He:	Are you mad at me?
She:	No, I'm not. Why?
He:	You won't talk to me.
She:	I'm too busy to talk.
He:	You don't seem to be too busy to talk to Jack.
She:	Jack was talking to *me*.
He:	I'm also talking to you!
She:	You don't talk, you whine!

3. Ask two students to take the different roles and to read the dialogue aloud.

4. Now, hand out – or project – the following skeleton of the dialogue:

He asked her if
She said that …. and asked him why.
He complained that
She replied that
He pointed out that
She explained that
He reminded her that
Cruelly, she told him that

5. Ask the class for ideas as to how they would complete the first and second lines. For example:

He asked her if *she was mad at him.*
She said that *she wasn't* and asked him why.

6. Use these examples to demonstrate three principles of reporting speech (when the reporting verbs are in the past), ie,

1. tense "backshift": *are* → *was*
2. pronoun shift: *you* → *she; me* → *him*
3. lack of inversion in questions: *are you mad* → *(if) she was mad*

7. Ask students, working in pairs, to complete the rest of the description of the conversation, using reported speech. Check this with the whole class. A possible version of the answer might be:

He asked her if *she was mad at him.*
She said that *she wasn't* and asked him why.
He complained that *she wouldn't talk to him.*
She replied that *she was too busy to talk.*
He pointed out that *she didn't seem to be too busy to talk to Jack.*
She explained that *Jack had been talking to her.*
He reminded her that *he was also talking to her.*
Cruelly, she told him that *he didn't talk, he whined.*

8. Ask students to cover up the original dialogue and/or mask it on the board. Then, working in pairs, they should try and reconstruct it, using the reported speech version as an aid.

CONSOLIDATION

1. Organise the class into pairs or small groups. Ask each group to write a short (6 to 8-line) dialogue, in direct speech, of a similar type to the one in *Discovery*, ie, of a couple either having an argument, or, after an argument, making up.

2. They then exchange their dialogues with another group and transpose these into reported speech.

3. The new versions of the dialogue are returned to the original group for checking and commentary.

USE

1. Organise the class into groups of three. Nominate a topic, such as *Daily routine* or *Free-time activities* or *Favourite movie.* Two students in each group then have a short conversation – half a minute is probably enough – while the third student listens.

2. Ask selected "listeners" to briefly report to the class on the conversation that they were the observers of, using reported speech.

3. Continue the activity, this time changing the topic, and the roles, so that there is a new listener in each group. Repeat a third time, so that everyone has had a chance to listen and report.

LEVEL
Intermediate +

TIME
50 minutes

EXTRAS
(Optional) class set of skeleton text A and jumbled text B

Section B

LEAD-IN ACTIVITIES
• Quotation from a young adult novel
Read out the following text to your students.

Jeff, a high school student, visits Ellen, a classmate, to apologise for his rude behaviour towards her at school.
'Hey, Ellen,' I said, '... listen Ellen, don't cry. Listen... I... I'm sorry. I didn't mean what I said.'
'Yes, you did,' she said. 'You did mean it.'
'No, I didn't,' I lied. 'It was just a lousy day for me. You know how it is sometimes. You have a lousy day, and you just say stupid things that you don't mean. Honestly, Ellen, I didn't mean it.'
Marilyn Sachs. *The Fat Girl*, Corgi Freeway 1987, p.45

• Personalising the topic
1. Talk about a situation in which you said something different from what you thought or felt.
2. Ask your students what the reason for your behaviour might have been and note their ideas on the board. For example:

   fear / not caring / not wanting to hurt /shyness / etc.

PRESENTATION OF MODEL TEXT
1. Ask your students to work in pairs at constructing a text from the skeleton below. Allow about five minutes.

Skeleton text A
I s _ _ _ I d _ _ _ ' _ c _ _ _,
b _ _ I d _ _ _ ' _ f _ _ _ _ g _ _ _ _ i _ _ _ t _ _ _,
I s _ _ _ t _ _ c _ _ _ _ _ w _ _ a g _ _ _ i _ _ _,
b _ _ I w _ _ _ ' _ s _ _ _ w _ _ _ _ _ _ I r _ _ _ _ _ f _ _ _ I _ _ _
g _ _ _ _,
a _ _ I _ _ _ _ I s _ _ _ t _ _ _ a d _ _ _ _ w _ _ f _ _ _ w _ _ _ m _
b _ _ I w _ _ t _ _ _ _ a _ _ w _ _ _ o _ _
a _ _ I h _ _ _ _ m _ _ _ _ _ f _ _ d _ _ _ _ t _ _ _ _ _
I r _ _ _ _ _ d _ _ _ ' _ w _ _ _ t _ d _ .

2. Re-form the class. Elicit the completions and add them onto the board.

Model text A
I said I didn't care,
but I didn't fancy going into town,
I said the cinema was a good idea,
but I wasn't sure whether I really felt like going,
and later I said that a drink was fine with me,
but I was tired and worn out
and I hated myself for doing things
I really didn't want to do.

• Interaction
1. Ask your students to write down key words for a situation in which what they said was different from what they thought.
2. Ask them to share their recollections in groups of four.

SECOND RECONSTRUCTION
1. Hand out copies of the jumbled text below.
2. Working individually, students put it in the correct order.

Variation
Put the text on an OHP or on the board for students to copy.

Jumbled text B
when she explained all the details,
when she showed me her new machine,
But I felt good about my lies
but I thought that
I said 'how interesting'
playing chess with a machine was awful.
because she is such a lovely girl.
but I thought that a computer was
I said 'wow'
I said 'marvellous'
when she played a game on the screen,
but I thought that the view from her room was nice.
the last thing I would buy for myself.

Model text B
I said 'how interesting'
when she showed me her new machine,
but I thought that a computer was
the last thing I would buy for myself.
I said 'marvellous'
when she explained all the details,
but I thought that the view from her room was nice.
I said 'wow'
when she played a game on the screen,
but I thought that
playing chess with a machine was awful.
But I felt good about my lies
because she is such a lovely girl.

TEXT CREATION
1. Following the model, your students write their own texts. Allow about fifteen minutes.
2. Students read their texts out loud.

LEVEL
Intermediate +

TIME
50–60 minutes

Section A

AIM
- to introduce *if*-clauses used to talk about unreal, non-past situations (the "second conditional")

DISCOVERY

1. If you have a projector, copy and project the following grid for a period of not more than 30 seconds. Tell the students to study it and to remember as many words as they can. Then turn it off and ask the students to write down the words they can remember, at first individually, and then comparing in pairs. If you don't have a projector, copy the grid, and distribute it face down. At a given signal, students turn it over and study it for 30 seconds. They then hide it, and write down the words they can remember.

black	young	short	big	good
weak	small	hot	north	tight
old	loose	south	white	right
bad	tall	cold	wrong	strong

2. Tell the students that the twenty words form ten pairs of opposites. Before you reveal the words again, ask if they can find the pairs. (This activity will help fill in some of the blanks in their memory.) Reveal the words again, for about 15 seconds, and allow them to amend their lists, both individually, and in pairs. Finally let them study the words at their leisure, to see if they have them all. Check that they have identified the ten pairs of opposites.

3. Now, ask the students to imagine a "topsy-turvy" world where everything is upside down and back-to-front. For example, say *Imagine if black was white. Or if old was young. Or if good was bad.* Ask the students to think silently about this for a short while. Elicit some ideas from the class, or prompt them by giving some examples of your own. For example, *If black was white, this would be a blackboard, not a whiteboard. If old was young, I would be younger than you. If good was bad, Olga would be a bad student!* etc.

4. Write some of these examples on the board. Draw attention to the use of the past tense form in the *if*-clause, used to express an unreal situation in an imaginary present. Point out, too, the use of the conditional *would* only in the main clause.

CONSOLIDATION

1. Ask the students, working in pairs or small groups, to come up with other examples of a topsy-turvy world, using adjectives from the grid in the *Discovery* stage. They should write these onto overhead transparencies, if available, or onto a poster-sized piece of paper

2. Collect the transparencies, or the posters, and display them. Correct any inaccuracies, but make sure you comment positively about evidence of the students' imagination and creativity.

USE

1. Describe an imaginary event in your life, for example how you would like to spend a forthcoming landmark birthday (your 30th, 40th, or 50th, let's say) or an anniversary. The description could be something like this:

I'd like to celebrate my Xth birthday in the mountains, just with a few friends and close family. I'd rent a house for a week, near a lake, and we'd all stay there – there'd be about 12 of us. During the day we'd go for long hikes or we'd go canoeing on the lake. In the evening we'd take turns to cook, and then we'd sit round the fire, and those who are a bit musical would play or sing. It would be quite simple; there would be no presents or speeches, but just a chance for people to spend some time together and feel unthreatened by the passage of time.

2. Invite the students to ask you questions about this event. Encourage them to ask questions beginning *Would you...?* where appropriate.

3. Allow the students time to imagine their own landmark event. They can then take turns to tell their partner about it, and to answer their partner's questions.

LEVEL
Intermediate +

TIME
40 minutes

EXTRAS
Class set of jumbled text; a few bilingual dictionaries

Section B

LEAD-IN ACTIVITIES

• Introducing a person

1. Describe the appearance and personality of someone you know well.
2. Read out a text along the lines of the model below to fit the person you have just described.

Model text
A person I like

If he was a colour, he'd be beige,
if he was a sound, he'd be a low hum,
if he was a smell, he'd be rain on a sunny day,
if he was an animal, he'd be a bear
and if he was food, he'd be a juicy steak.

• Collecting words

1. Write a grid on the board and ask everyone to note at least five words for each heading on a sheet of paper.

COLOURS	SOUNDS	SMELLS	ANIMALS	FOOD

Encourage use of bilingual dictionaries. Allow about three or four minutes.

2. Elicit the students' words and write them on the board.

PRESENTATION OF MODEL TEXT

1. Hand out copies of the jumbled text.
2. Ask your students to put the right endings with the right beginnings.
3. Read out the correct version.

Jumbled text
A person I don't like

If he was a colour, he'd be a spider.
if he was a sound, he'd be porridge,
if he was a smell, he'd be a dirty grey,
if he was an animal, he'd be burning tyres,
and if he was food, he'd be the hissing of a snake.

Model text
A person I don't like

If he was a colour, he'd be a dirty grey,
if he was a sound, he'd be the hissing of a snake,
if he was a smell, he'd be burning tyres,
if he was an animal, he'd be a spider,
and if he was food, he'd be porridge.

TEXT CREATION

Ask your students to write their own texts. They can write about a good friend, someone in their family, people they know from the media, etc. Tell them not to forget to give their text a title. The following text was written by a fourteen-year-old student:

A person I don't like

If he was a colour, he'd be a dirty yellow,
if he was a sound, he'd be the grunting of a pig,
if he was a smell, he'd be petrol,
if he was an animal, he'd be an elephant,
and if he was food, he'd be a fat chicken.

4.6 REPORTED COMMANDS

LEVEL
Lower intermediate +

TIME
30 minutes

Section A

AIM
– to introduce reported commands

DISCOVERY

1. Deliver five or six commands to the class, such as *Stand up, turn around, turn around again, put your left hand up, raise your right leg, jump,* and *sit down again.* You may need to demonstrate the commands by doing them yourself at the same time as you say them.

2. Ask the class, *Can you remember the instructions?* When students start to recall them, encourage them to use the sentence frame: *You told us to....* Write it on the board.

3. Announce that you are going to give the class more instructions. This time precede some of the instructions with *Don't...* as in *Stand up, don't turn around, put your right hand up, don't jump...* etc.

4. Repeat stage 2 above: this time, model and write up the sentence frame: *You told us not to...*

CONSOLIDATION

1. Copy and distribute – or project – the following table:

	told		(not)	
The teacher	told	me	(not)	to talk.
Jack's father		you		to be quiet.
Jill's mother		him		to cheat.
My friend		her		to laugh.
Another student		us		to be good.
I		them		to eat up.
				to be silly.

2. Read out the first of the following sentences. After each sentence ask if anyone in the class can report the sentence, using a sentence constructed from the table. For example, "*Be quiet," said another student to me.* → *Another student told me to be quiet.*

   1. "Be quiet", said another student to me.
   2. "Eat up," her mother said to Jill.
   3. "Don't talk," said the teacher to the students.
   4. "Don't cheat," my friend said to me.
   5. "Be good," said Jack's father to Jack.
   6. "Don't laugh," I said to my sister.
   7. "Don't be silly," the teacher said to us.
   8. "Cheat," said Jack's father to Jill.

3. Read out the rest of the sentences, pausing after each one. The students should write down the reported version of each one, and then compare their answers in pairs. If necessary read out some – or all – of the sentences again.

4. When you have checked the task, ask students, in pairs, to do the same. That is, one student says a sentence using direct speech and the other responds by reporting it. The sentences can be based on the table, or they can be created by adding new elements into its columns.

USE

1. Write the following questions on the board: *Why? What happened? What did you do?*

2. Tell the class about something that you were once told to do, or not to do. Use this sentence frame: *Once/The other day, [...] told me to...* or *Once/The other day [...] told me not to....* For example: *Once, my headmaster told me to cut my hair.* Or, *The other day my doctor told me not to worry.* Encourage the students to ask you questions about this event, using the questions on the board as starters.

3. Ask each student to write two or three statements using the same model. In pairs or small groups, they take turns to read their statements aloud, and to answer the questions of their classmates.

LEVEL
Lower intermediate +

TIME
40 minutes

EXTRAS
Class set of text A

Section B

LEAD-IN ACTIVITIES
• Mime the action
1. Ask your students to work in groups of four. They decide on four actions to mime, eg, *eating spaghetti, riding a bike, playing table tennis*, etc. Allow about three minutes.
2. Re-form your class. Ask one student from each group to come to the front of the class. One after the other, ask them to start miming. The other students try to guess, for example:

   Are you playing the guitar?
   Are you making pizza?

PRESENTATION OF MODEL TEXTS
1. Hand out copies of model text A and ask your students to read it to themselves.

   Model text A
   I told him not to open the door with a hammer,
   I told him not to sit on the vase,
   I told him not to try to catch the
   birds in the cherry tree,
   I told him not to eat the cactus,
   I told him not to feed the cat with the goldfish.
   Phew! Isn't he a bloody nuisance.

2. Say you are going to read a similar but different text twice. Tell your students not to write anything down until you have finished reading it out. Their task is to change text A according to what they hear (text B).
3. Read model text B twice.
4. Students read out their new version. Comment on accuracy.
5. Read text B out again. Students compare their texts with text B and correct.

   Model text B
   I told him not to open the can with a spoon,
   I told him not to eat the flowers in the vase,
   I told him not to jump down from the balcony,
   I told him not to drink the perfume,
   I told him not to cut the cat's claws.
   Phew! Isn't he a bloody nuisance.

• Making lists
1. Students work in groups of four to write ten sentences of the pattern:

   I/She/He told him/her/me not to... (paint the kitchen with honey)

If there are five groups, each group makes five copies of their list of sentences, if there are six groups, each writes six copies and so on.

2. Each group hands one copy to each of the other groups and keeps one for themselves.

TEXT CREATION

1. Choosing from the raw material contained in their various lists, each group writes a text structured like text B. But encourage them to think of their own ending.
2. They then read their texts out loud.

This text was written by a fourteen-year-old in his fourth year of English.

*I told her not to put jam into her
enemy's hair,
I told her not to water the flowers
with our best wine,
I told her not to lock her little
brother into the lion's cage,
I told her not to put poisonous snakes
into her parents' bedroom,
I told her not to burn down the school,
but she didn't listen and now
she writes postcards from a place
right in the centre of the Sahara.*

Variation

If you work with adults you may want to use the following model text:

*I told him not to try
to repair the washing machine,
I told him not to forget
to keep the dog on the lead,
I told him not to water
the cacti every day,
I told him not to mow
the lawn at midnight.
And do you know what he said?
'Didn't I do nicely?'*

4.7 *COULD* FOR POSSIBILITY

LEVEL
Lower intermediate +

TIME
30 minutes

Section A

AIM
– to introduce *could* for hypothetical ability and possibility

DISCOVERY

1. Write the following gapped sentences on the board, and ask the students, discussing in pairs, to think of *one word* that could complete all the gaps:

    a. *What ____ I buy with 10 cents?*
    b. *There's someone at the door. Who ____ it be?*
    c. *When I was younger, I _____ run up the stairs without stopping.*
    d. *With her talent, she ____ be famous one day.*
    e. *I ____ do a lot of things with a million euros.*
    f. *Excuse me, _____ you turn the music down, please?*
    g. *I'm sorry, I _____n't hear you.*
    h. *Take an umbrella. It _____ rain.*

2. Establish that the missing word is *could*. Now, ask the students to identify those examples that refer to present or future possibility – ie, a, b, d, e and h. Point out that, in some of these cases – eg a, b, and possibly e – *could* is interchangeable with *can,* but that *could* adds an element of uncertainty. In d and h, *can* is much less likely.

CONSOLIDATION

1. Copy – or project – the following matching exercise. Ask the students, working in pairs, to make the most likely matches between the sentences in each column:

1. *Take a sweater.*	a. *You could start a fire.*
2. *He's very funny.*	b. *She could be the next President.*
3. *Don't play with matches.*	c. *He could be a comedian.*
4. *Buy a lottery ticket.*	d. *It could be expensive.*
5. *She's very popular.*	e. *It could get cold.*
6. *Take a book.*	f. *Then I could fix it.*
7. *All I need is a screwdriver.*	g. *You could win.*
8. *Have you got your credit card?*	h. *It could be a long wait.*

2. Check the task in open class. The answers are: 1 – e; 2 – c; 3 – a; 4 – g; 5 – b; 6 – h; 7 – f; 8 – d.

3. Ask the students to imagine a situation in which some of these sentences might have been uttered. For example, *Take a sweater. It could get cold.* = two people getting ready to go to a football match in winter.

4. Now, ask the students to mask the right-hand column of the matching exercise. Working in pairs, they should try and reconstruct the sentences with *could* that match the prompts in the left-hand column.

USE

1. On the board, write the following:

   this evening
   tomorrow
   next week
   next month
   next summer
   before I die

2. Demonstrate the activity, by telling the class a plan or wish that you have for one of the above time periods. For example, *I want to visit Egypt next summer.* Encourage them to respond with a statement beginning *That could....,* *It could...,* or *You could...* For example, *That could be exciting. It could be hot. You could take a boat up the Nile....*

3. In pairs, students take turns to do the same.

LEVEL
Lower intermediate +

TIME
40 minutes

EXTRAS
Class set of time-phrases list and photo

Section B

PREPARATION
Make enough copies of text A for each group of four students. Cut each copy into one-line strips. Copy a photo like the one below for each pair of students.

LEAD-IN ACTIVITY
• **Picture associations**
1. Ask your students to work in pairs. Hand out a photocopy of a photograph similar to the one below to each pair.

2. Ask the students to jot down, on one sheet of paper, as many words as they can that they associate with the picture.

• **Structuring word fields**
1. Ask the pairs to shout their words to you. Write them on the board.

2. Rub out the words. Then, getting students to help you recall what was on the board, rewrite the words in some kind of principled arrangement. For example, parts of speech in columns of different colours or in mind-map form below. Leave this on the board as a help for the students in the writing phase.

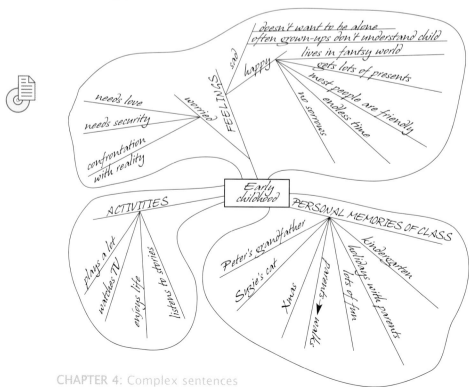

CHAPTER 4: Complex sentences

• Thinking back
1. Tell your learners about a childhood dream (eg, wish for the future) you had.
2. Give each student a copy of the list below. Ask everyone to write down key words for dreams they had at the times of their lives mentioned in the list. Depending on the age of your learners, you might have to adapt the list.

Dream
Last year
Three years ago
Five years ago
Ten years ago
Fifteen yars ago
Twenty years ago

• Group reflection
Ask your students to talk about their dreams in groups. In a class of lower intermediate learners it might be helpful to write the following language on the board:

Last year		*having...*
Three years ago		*getting ...*
Five years ago	*I dreamt of*	*winning ...*
Ten years ago		*being ...*
Fifteen years ago		*being able to ...*
Twenty years ago		*making ...*

PRESENTATION AND RECONSTRUCTION OF MODEL TEXT
1. Keeping the same groups, hand out your strips of the model text.
2. Ask them to put the strips in order as you read the text. (Read it twice.)

Model text
With a lot more money
I could buy
a horse and a hot air balloon.
With a lot more time
I could build myself a tree house
in the old oak.
What a pity
that I don't have
more spare time
and a lot of money.
Or am I just lucky
to have what I have?

TEXT CREATION

Ask your learners to write their own texts following the model text. If you think it necessary, write the following skeleton on the board:

Skeleton text
With _____
_____ *could* _____ *and* _____ ,
with _____
_____ *could* _____ *and* _____ ,
What a _____
that _____
and _____
Or _____
_____ *to* _____ ?

TEXT SHARING

Collect the finished texts and mount them, possibly along with some photos, on poster paper for display on the wall. The students stroll about and read the texts.

ACKNOWLEDGEMENT

The technique of mind mapping comes from Tony Buzan. See Buzan 1974 for more on this form of representation.

4.8 *I WISH I* + PAST

LEVEL
Lower intermediate +

TIME
40 minutes

Section A

AIM
– to introduce *I wish* + past tense to talk about present wishes

DISCOVERY
1. Draw the picture below on the board, or project it. Draw a thought bubble above the person's head and write into it *I wish I ...*

2. Ask your students for various completions of the sentence. For example, *I wish I had a gun. I wish I could run faster. I wish I was dreaming....* If the students don't come up with any ideas, prompt them by saying, for example, *gun, run, dream...*

3. Write the sentences on the board. Establish that the person is making wishes about *now,* (ie, the present), but draw attention to the use of the past tense verbs: *had, could, was...* Explain that this is a kind of hypothetical present.

CONSOLIDATION
1. Present the following table on a poster, or project it, and ask the class to study it silently for about a minute.

I wish	*I had* *I was / were* *I lived* *I could* *I wasn't / weren't* *I didn't*	*in another country / play the piano /* *stronger / tidier / so careless / so tired /* *solve my problems / more time /* *alone / with my girl (woman, guy, man) /* *a flat of my own / a new bike / a new television /* *help him(her) / live in ... / remember it /* *understood it / a good friend / in love / ill /* *understand it / live in peace / a coward /* *have to do it / have to leave /*

2. Mask the table, and ask students to write down as many grammatically correct sentences as they can remember. Allow them to check in pairs.

3. Invite individual students to read out their sentences. When half of the class have read their sentences, ask the remaining students each to choose one particularly meaningful sentence from their own list. Ask them to say that sentence out loud.

4. Comment on individual sentences by reacting in a natural way. For example:

Student:	*I wish I lived in another country.*
Teacher:	*Where would you like to live?*
Student:	*In ....*

USE

1. Prepare sets of about ten to fifteen cards, one for each group of three to five students. For children, the set can be animals, eg, *a fish, a frog, a cat, an elephant, an eagle, a butterfly, a bear, an albatross, a seal, a rabbit...* For adults, the set could be the names of famous people, such as sports personalities, actors, musicians, politicians.

2. Organise the class into groups and give each group a set of cards which they place face down. Each student in turn takes a card, and makes a statement beginning either *I wish I was* or *I'm glad I'm not* [name of animal or person on card] and then gives a reason. The reason cannot be repeated in a succeeding turn. If the rest of the group judges the sentence to be well-formed and to make sense the student gets two points if the sentence began *I wish I was ..* and one point if the sentence began *I'm glad I'm not...* They keep playing until all the cards have been used.

3. At the end of the game, ask individuals from each group to report to the class some of the more interesting sentences that were produced.

LEVEL
Lower intermediate +

TIME
45 minutes

EXTRAS
Class set of worksheets;
substitution table on OHP
transparency or big sheet
of poster paper

Section B

PRESENTATION OF MODEL TEXTS
1. Form groups of three.
2. Hand out a copy of the worksheet below to each student. The students work together to try to fill in the missing words.

WORKSHEET

Text A *I wish I had more _____ .*
I wish I wasn't _____ .

I wish my fingers _____ quiet
and I wish I wasn't thinking of
_____ my hands
round the neck of the fat man
who had just the _____ queue.

blow up /noise /jumped /
patience / planning /
nervous / interesting / lose /
punctual / crying /
thumbs / animal /
would keep / listening /
putting / raising /
voice / laughing

Text B *I wish / wasn't so _____ .*
I wish I had the _____ to talk to her.
I wish I could hold my _____ up high.
I wish I wasn't feeling so _____
like a kitten
_____ in the rain.

jumped / tired / knee /
happy / nervous /
courage / kept /
raising / head / staring /
crying / small / lost /
putting / laughing

• **Comparison of texts**
1. Some of the students read their versions to the whole class.
2. Read out the versions below. Tell everyone to check their texts against the originals.

Model text A
I wish I had more patience.
I wish I wasn't nervous.
I wish my fingers would keep quiet
and I wish I wasn't thinking of
putting my hands
round the neck of the fat man
who has just jumped the queue.

Model text B
I wish I wasn't so nervous.
I wish I had the courage to talk to her.
I wish I could hold my head up high
and I wish I wasn't feeling so small
like a kitten
lost in the rain.

NOTE

In the texts above *were/weren't* could be used instead of *was/wasn't*.

TEXT CREATION

1. Learners write their own texts using those above as models. Make it clear to them that they should follow the same grammatical framework *(I wish ...)*, but add their own ideas and ending.
2. They can then read their texts out loud.

REPORTED SPEECH

LEVEL
Intermediate +

TIME
40 minutes

Section A

AIM
– to introduce reported speech with a focus on the past

DISCOVERY
1. Copy and distribute – or project – these pictures and these speech bubbles.

1 _____   2 _____   3 _____

2. Ask the students to match the speech bubbles to the pictures and to compare their answers with a neighbour. Check the answers in open class. The most likely answers are:

a *She said she hasn't been feeling well.*

b *She said she hadn't been feeling well.*

c *She says she hasn't been feeling well.*

3. Ask students if they can explain the choice of tense, both of *says/said* and *hasn't/hadn't,* in each case. They can discuss this briefly in pairs.

4. Elicit the students' ideas, and establish that the choice of tense depends on both the time of "saying" and the time of "not feeling well". When reporting speech, the choice of tense depends on the relationship between (a) the present moment, (b) the moment of reporting, and (c) the time of the events that are being reported. In (1) they are all the same, ie, *now.* In (2) the time of the event is the same as now, but the time of reporting is *then.* In (3) they are all different, ie *now, then* and *before then.*

CONSOLIDATION
1. Copy and hand out – or project – the following jumbled dialogue. Alternatively, copy it and cut it up into its individual lines, so that the students can physically manipulate it. You will need one set of jumbled lines for each group of three students.

Well, I downloaded it myself.
You told me you had written it yourself.
What's wrong with it?
What's the problem?
No, you didn't. I found it on the Internet.
It's about your English homework.
I did.

The actual order is the following:

What's the problem?
It's about your English homework.
What's wrong with it?
You told me you had written it yourself.
I did.
No, you didn't. I found it on the Internet.
Well, I downloaded it myself.

2. Once the students have ordered the dialogue, ask them to imagine the context in which it occurred.

3. Ask the students, in pairs, to write, rehearse, and perform a similar dialogue based on one of these situations:

   1. An employer discovers an employee has lied in his or her job interview.
   2. A parent discovers their child was lying about what they did last Saturday night.
   3. A customer complains to a car salesman about the car that he or she bought, which was supposed to be new.

USE
1. Tell the class the story of how someone misled you, or lied to you, or tricked you in some way. For example:

Once, I rented a room in a flat. The person who rented it to me told me he owned the flat. In fact, I soon found out that he didn't. He was sub-letting it. What's more, he didn't have any money himself. He was depending on me to pay all the rent...

2. Invite the students to ask you more questions about the situation.

3. Ask students to think of a something similar that happened to them or to someone they know. In pairs or groups of three they take turns to tell their story. Encourage the listeners to ask questions about it.

4. Ask for volunteers to tell some of the best stories to the whole class.

LEVEL
Intermediate +

TIME
60 minutes

EXTRAS
Several copies of the model text

Section B

LEAD-IN ACTIVITIES
• Spot the lies
Write some statements about yourself on the board and get your students to decide whether they think they are true or lies. You score a point when the students consider something that is true to be a lie and vice versa. If the group cannot decide, take a majority vote. For example:

Teacher: My grandmother was born in Ireland.
When I was a child, we kept chickens in our cellar.
I once travelled round Cornwall on a tandem bike.
My favourite series on TV is ...
I hate spinach and would never eat it.

• What's your score?
1. Tell the students to pick a partner they do not know very well.
2. Both write down five sentences which they then read out to their partner, who guesses whether the sentence is true or a lie. The one who guesses scores a point for each correct guess. For example:

Student 1:   When I was a child, I had a cat as a pet.
Student 2:   True.
Student 1:   No, it's a lie, I always wanted to have one but I was never allowed to keep a pet. (No point for Student 2)

3. Get the class into a circle. Each student reports their score and gives just one example of something they guessed wrong. It might be helpful to write the following on the board.

Hisako/Alain said she/he	*had...*
	had met...
	had been to ...

I thought it was a lie (true), but it's true (a lie).

PRESENTATION OF MODEL TEXT
1. Put three to six copies of the model text up on the walls around your room. There should be at least one copy for each three students. Ask your students to copy it onto sheets of paper which they must leave at their desks or tables. That is, since the text is not in large lettering, everyone has to get up, read part of the text, go back to their seat, write down what they remember, go back to the text and read a bit more, and so on.

Model text
He told us he had an uncle in Japan
and he said
they had spent their holidays in
Hawaii

and he added
that his father had bought a Porsche
and he told us that they had a house
as big as the school building
but then we found out
that he was just like us,
but a liar.

2. When everyone has finished, read out the text. Students check their copies. (Perhaps, as you read, stroll around and check that everyone is producing an accurate copy.)

ACKNOWLEDGEMENT
We learnt this technique from Mario Rinvolucri.

TEXT CREATION
Everyone writes their own text based on the model and presents it to the class.

• Lies don't pay
1. Tell your class about a time you or somebody else told a lie and regretted having done so.
2. Write the key words from the story on the board.
3. Allow a few minutes for the class to think about a time somebody lied. It does not matter whether they experienced the situation themselves or whether they heard/read about it or saw it in a film.
4. Tell them to write about the situation using key words only. Give an example.
5. Ask a student for his or her key words. Write them on the board. Invite the others to flesh out the story individually or in groups.

Variation
If you work with adults you may want to use the following model text:

My new acquaintance told me
he loved parachuting
he said he went to the theatre
at least once a week
he added that he had played in an
orchestra some time ago
and he mentioned
that he had travelled all over the
world,
but he forgot to tell me
that all these things
had only happened inside his head.

4.10 IF- CLAUSE + PAST

LEVEL
Intermediate +

TIME
45 minutes

Section A

AIM
– to introduce the second conditional, statements and questions

DISCOVERY

1. Write the following question on the board: *If someone gave you a magic lamp, what would you wish for?* Check the meaning of *magic lamp* and *wish* (by reference to Aladdin, perhaps). Ask the students to think silently for half a minute. Elicit ideas from volunteers. As they suggest things – such as *a trip to London*, or *a mountain bike* – reformulate these in the form of complete sentences: *Nino would wish for a trip to London. Carla would wish for a mountain bike.*

2. Write some of the students' ideas on to the board, in the form of a complete second conditional sentence:

   If someone gave Carla a magic lamp, she'd wish for a mountain bike.

3. Establish that this is an imaginary situation. Draw attention to the past-tense verb in the *if*-clause = the hypothetical present. And point out that *she'd* is a contraction for *she would*.

4. Ask each student to write a full sentence about their own wish, using the pattern: *If someone gave me … , I'd…*

CONSOLIDATION

1. Copy and hand out – or project – the following table:

If	someone I liked someone I didn't like someone I didn't know	asked me for… asked me to … told me to…. called me a … invited me to … offered me …. refused to …	I'd I wouldn't	feel… be… tell them to… say…. try to.. pretend to …

2. Construct an example sentence using the table. For example, *If someone I didn't know offered me money, I'd be suspicious.* Invite the students to ask you why, and give a reason.

3. Ask the students to do the same, ie, to construct four or five sentences based on the table, working individually. Then, in pairs or small groups, they take turns to read them to one another, and to ask further questions about them.

4. Ask individual students to read one or two sentences out to the class.
USE
1. Write the following rubric on the board:

	brave	
	generous	
How	honest	are you?
	adventurous	
	romantic	

2. Tell the class that they are going to conduct a survey in order to answer one of these questions. First they will need to devise multiple choice questions. Give an example for *brave:*
If you saw someone being mugged in the street, would you
a. *call the police?*
b. *go and help them?*
c. *run away?*

3. Organise the class into groups, and assign an adjective from the rubric in Step 1 to each group. Ask each group to prepare four or five questions for their adjective. Assign a letter (A, B, C, etc) to each person in each group. Re-group the class by asking all the As in the class to sit together, and all the Bs, and so on. Once they are re-grouped, they take turns to ask their questions to each member of the group, and to note down the answers.

4. Students now go back to their original groups, and report their findings. They then prepare a summary of their survey, consisting of sentences such as:

If they saw someone being mugged, most people said they would call the police...

Individual students from each group then read out their summaries to the class.

LEVEL
Intermediate +

TIME
40–50 minutes

EXTRAS
None

Section B

PRESENTATION OF MODEL TEXT

1. Read out the model text twice. Your students should not write anything down.
2. After the second reading, they try to reconstruct the text individually.
3. In pairs or groups of three, students compare notes. Each group/pair agrees on a full version.
4. They read their texts back to you.
5. If there are discrepancies from the model text, read it again to allow for another check.

Model text
If they asked me to cut my hair
I'd grow it long.
If they told me to tidy up my room
I'd make a mess.
If they ordered me to study harder
I'd burn my books.
But the trouble is
that they leave me alone
and I hate them for that.

TEXT CREATION

1. Give your students the following skeleton text and ask them to write their own texts. Instead of *I/me* the students may, of course, use *he/him*, *she/her*, *we/us*, *they/them*.

Skeleton text
If they asked me _____
I'd _____
If they told me _____
I'd _____
If they ordered me _____
I'd _____
But the trouble is
that _____
and I _____

2. Publication of texts.

Variation
If you work with adults you may want to use the following model text:

If she asked me
to give up cigarettes,
I'd start smoking cigars.

If she told me
to help with the washing up,
I'd break all the plates.
If she asked me
to do the shopping,
I'd spend the money in a pub.
If she asked me
to stop eating chips
I'd gorge myself on them.
But she accepts me
the way I am
and that drives me mad.

4.11 GERUND

LEVEL
Intermediate +

TIME
30 minutes

Section A

AIM
– to introduce gerunds (*-ing* forms) as clause subjects

DISCOVERY
1. Write the following sentences on the board:

   Making grammar mistakes is OK.
   Speaking English is the best way of learning it.
   Learning a language is like learning to ride a bike.

2. Ask the students if they agree with these statements. They can discuss them in pairs first, but there should also be an open class discussion. So long as students are showing interest in the topic, let this discussion continue.

3. Use the sentences to highlight the use of *-ing* forms as subjects of the sentence. Ask the students what the subject of each sentence is, ie, *Making grammar mistakes, Speaking English, Learning a language*. Point out what these subjects have in common – they are all formed from verb + object combinations, where the verb is in the *-ing* form (also called a gerund).

4. Elicit some other possible statements about language learning, beginning with *-ing* forms. Provide prompts if necessary, eg, *Learning vocabulary... Passing exams ... Being corrected.... Doing homework ....*

CONSOLIDATION
1. Hand out (or project) the following fragmented sayings and ask the students, working individually and then comparing in pairs, to match the two halves.

Knowing that something is true	*is better than never trying at all.*
Embracing uncertainty	*is like halving it.*
Trying to do something and failing	*is better than arriving there.*
Sharing a problem with someone	*is not the same as experiencing it.*
Learning a new language	*is the first step to inner peace.*
Travelling towards your destination	*is like making a new friend.*

2. Check the task, including any unfamiliar vocabulary. The expected answers are:

Knowing that something is true	*is not the same as experiencing it.*
Embracing uncertainty	*is the first step to inner peace.*
Trying to do something and failing	*is better than never trying at all.*
Sharing a problem with someone	*is like halving it.*
Learning a new language	*is like making a new friend.*
Travelling towards your destination	*is better than arriving there.*

3. Organise students into pairs. One of each pair masks the above table, while the other reads the first half of one of the sayings (such as *Learning a new language...*). Their partner tries to complete it. After they have attempted all six sayings, they should change roles.

USE

1. Take one of the sayings from the Consolidation section and ask students if they agree with it, and why, or why not. Ask them if they can think of a real-life example that might prove or disprove the saying.

2. Organise the class into small groups and ask them to continue discussing the sayings. Do they all agree that they are true? If not, why not? Can they think of real-life examples?

3. Ask a spokesperson from each group to report to the class some of the more interesting points that came up in their discussion.

LEVEL
Intermediate +

TIME
2 lessons of 40 minutes each

EXTRAS
Class sets of the table below, the cut up model text and a copy of the skeleton text for each pair; 30 slips of adhesive paper (or use Blu-Tack); felt-tip pens; visuals (photos, drawings) for collages

Section B

PREPARATION

Photocopy the model text: you need one text per group of four learners. Cut the text up line by line. Write words (see Presentation of Model Text, Step 2) on slips of paper, one word per slip, written rather small so that the students have to get up if they want to read them.

Lesson one

The aim of this activity is to make students aware of sensory areas and their own use of and preferences for certain ones.

LEAD-IN ACTIVITIES

1. Tell your students that different people frequently call to mind very different kinds of sensory experiences when a word makes an impression on them. Thus a word like *bell* might have a very strong visual impact on a person, who may literally *see* a colour picture of a bell when they 'think' of this word. Whereas another person, might actually *hear* the sound of the church bell of the village in which he used to live years ago. A third person might actually have the *feeling* of touching the metal surface of a bell. And there are people who may have two or more different kinds of such vivid sensory memories at the same time.

2. Give each student a grid (below).

3. Tell them that you are going to read them a list of words (see Step 4). They should write each word in the column on the left and tick the sensory area(s) that they link the word with.

word	visual (seeing)	auditory (hearing)	kinaesthetic (feeling, touching, moving)	gustatory (tasting)	olfactory (smelling)
bell					

4. Read out the following words to your class (or any words you want):

> *wind – bunch of flowers – beefsteak –*
> *modern painting – mushroom – lake – bike –*
> *mother–father–belt–pop music–cat*
> *chocolate bar*

5. Ask your students to compare their results in groups. You could write the following guiding questions on the board:

Which word(s) mostly triggered off the same sensory memories in the group?
Which word(s) triggered off the most different sensory memories in the group?
From your results, would you say you are the kind of person who experiences most through what you see, what you hear or through what you can touch or feel?
How far do your findings correspond to what you expected?

• Stem sentences
Present the following prompts and ask your students to write sentences and read them out later. They might wish to include some of the nouns from the grid above but they should also use other words. For example, *Smelling horses makes me think of Western films.*

Listening to	
Hearing	
Watching	
Seeing	*makes me think of...*
Feeling	*brings back memories of...*
Touching	
Smelling	
Tasting	

PRESENTATION OF MODEL TEXT
1. Form pairs and give each a copy of the skeleton text below.

Skeleton text
Listening to _____
talking about the _____
you wanted to _____ and never _____
makes me _____
of the _____ that I wanted to write
and never _____
It also brings back _____ of _____
I wanted to _____ better
and never _____
I _____ if I will ever
say the _____ to you
that I'd _____ to say.

2. Stick slips of paper on the walls of your room. Each slip should bear one of the following words:

get to know	*like*	*song*
memories	*things*	*truth*
wonder	*did*	*book*
think	*did*	*say*
you	*letters*	*intended*

cross	summer holidays	make
finished	chocolate pudding	tasks
bamboo bridge	have	happy
people	poem	sing

3. Get your students to complete the text by walking around the classroom searching for the words they need. Tell the students that there are more slips than gaps.

4. Ask the pairs to read out loud the texts they have created.

Lesson two
PRESENTATION OF MODEL TEXT
Read out the text below just once.

Model text
Listening to you
talking about the bamboo bridge
you wanted to cross and never did
makes me think
of the letters that I wanted to write
and never finished.
It also brings back memories of people
I wanted to get to know better
and never did.
I wonder if I will ever
say the things to you
that I'd like to say.

RECONSTRUCTION OF MODEL TEXT
1. Arrange your learners in groups.
2. Hand out the cut-up model text to each group.
3. Ask your learners to unjumble the strips.

TEXT CREATION
1. Write down the following words on the board.

Listening to ... (Hearing ... / Watching ...)
makes ... of
It also brings back memories of ...
I wonder if ...

2. Ask your learners to write a text based on the model.

PRESENTATION OF TEXT
1. Ask your students to create a visual (collage/drawing etc.) which they think fits the text they have created.
2. Display the texts and the visuals in class.

4.12 RELATIVE PRONOUNS *WHO, WHOSE*

LEVEL
Intermediate +

TIME
30 minutes

Section A

AIM
- to introduce the relative pronouns *who* and *whose* in defining relative clauses.

DISCOVERY

1. Write the following question on the board, checking any unfamiliar vocabulary, and ask students to think of the answer:

    What do you call a man who has a seagull on his head?

When the students have exhausted their ideas, tell them the answer *Cliff*. If necessary, explain the joke, ie, a cliff is a high rock with a steep side by the sea, and it is also a man's name.

2. Do the same for this joke:

    What do you call a woman whose hair is purple? (*Di*).

3. Use these jokes to illustrate the relative pronouns *who* and *whose* Show how *who* takes the place of the subject pronoun *he*.

    What do you call a man – he has a seagull on his head?
    What do you call a man who has a seagull on his head?

And that *whose* takes the place of the possessive adjective *her* (or *his*)

    What do you call a woman – her hair is purple?
    What do you call a woman whose hair is purple?

CONSOLIDATION

1. Hand out – or project – the following *jokes*, whose answers have been jumbled. It will help if you read out the column of answer first asking the students to listen carefully for clues in their pronunciation. Ask the students, working in pairs, to match the questions with the answers. Allow students to use dictionaries if they are available.

What do you call a man whose hair is cut short?	*Matt*
What do you call a man who floats on water?	*Mike*
What do you call a man who is very honest?	*Claude*
What do you call a man who has a paper bag on his head?	*Rob*
What do you call a man whose face is scratched?	*Sean*
What do you call a man whose voice is very loud?	*Frank*
What do you call a man who lies on the floor?	*Russel*
What do you call a man who steals things?	*Bob*

2. Check the task, asking the students to explain the jokes, if they can, and explaining them yourself, if they can't. (A *mat* lies on the floor; *mike* is short for microphone; if someone has been *clawed* they have been scratched; to *rob* is to steal; if someone has been *shorn* their hair has been cut short (but note that the pronunciation of *shorn* and *Sean* is the same only in standard British English); if someone is *frank* they are honest; a paper bag *rustles;* and things *bob* when they float on water.)

3. Ask students to cover the questions, and then, working in pairs, to try to reconstruct them from memory, using the answers as clues.

4. Ask the students if they can invent some jokes of their own, of the same type. To help, here are some more names that have other meanings (ie, they are homographs or homophones): *Mark, Pat, Bill, Will, Jack, Doug, Rod, Herb, Earnest,* and *Gail, Carol, Mona, Eve, Joy, Shelley.*

USE

1. Write the following table on the board:

I have a	friend brother sister etc	who... whose...
I know a	person someone somebody	

2. Demonstrate the task by constructing a true sentence based on the table. For example, *I have a friend who lives in a lighthouse....*

3. Pause at this point, and say nothing until a student volunteers a question. Note that you needn't *ask* for a question: your silence will be sufficient. Answer the student's question and wait for more to emerge.

4. Ask the students to construct their own true sentences using the table and to write these down. Then ask for a volunteer to come and sit in a seat at the front of the class, and to read their sentence aloud. They should then answer any questions that are directed at them (or, if they don't wish to answer a particular question, should simply say *No comment).* When their topic has been exhausted, ask for another student to come forward, and so on.

LEVEL
Intermediate +

TIME
50 minutes

EXTRAS
A cassette of soft,
meditative music

Section B

LEAD-IN ACTIVITIES
• A person I'd like to get to know
1. Ask your students to write down the name of a person they would like to get to know. Allow two or three minutes.
2. Ask them for the names they have come up with, write them on the board and ask them why they would like to get to know these people.

• A daydream
1. Invite your students to accompany you on a short trip. Tell them to sit comfortably with their backs straight. Begin to play some soft meditative music and guide them through a visualisation, for example:

I want you to imagine that you are sitting in an aeroplane ... the plane is taking off and you lean back in your comfy seat .. the plane is going higher and higher and you can see the blue sky ... you relax and lean back and dream ... and after some time you can feel the plane slowly going down and down until you feel it touch the ground and come to a standstill.

When you now get off the plane, you can see this marvellous beach with palm trees right in front of you. There is a small path which you follow down to the beach. You can feel the sand under your feet, the warmth of the sun on your skin and you hear the wind in the palm trees and the waves of the ocean. And there, right on the beach, a person is looking out at the sea, and when this person turns round you see that it is someone you have wanted to get to know for a long time. And you both sit down in the warm sand and begin to talk. Take all the time you need for your talk...

(Allow two minutes)

... Now as the sun goes down, you realise that the time has come for you to say good-bye, and you slowly walk back along the little path to the aeroplane that is waiting for you. And you get on and it slowly takes off and safely takes you back to our classroom here. And while you are slowly coming back you very clearly remember the person you got to know on the beach in that foreign country. Come slowly back now and open your eyes with a feeling of freshness and joy.

2. Ask your students to share what they experienced, in pairs. Some might even be willing to share with the whole group.

Variation
1. Suggest that everyone writes down key words about their experience during the creative visualisation.

2. Form pairs. Student A tries to guess from the key words who Student B met, what they talked about and so on. B comments on the accuracy of A's guesses. Then B guesses about A.

PRESENTATION AND RECONSTRUCTION OF MODEL TEXT
1. Display the model text. Omit all occurrences of *who* and *whose.*
2. Elicit the missing words.
3. Read the text out loud.
4. Cover up or rub out words of your choice (eg, all the verbs).
5. Elicit a reconstruction of the text. Do this three or four times. Delete different words each time.
6. Leave more and more gaps until no prompts are left and students are repeating the whole text from memory.

Model text
I'd like to get to know
a woman
who has golden eyes
who wears snakes as necklaces
whose pet is a toad
whose friends are sorcerers
and who,
if I want her to,
slips into a bottle
I keep at my bedside.

TEXT CREATION
1. Display a skeleton of the model text. Students write their own texts.

Skeleton text
I'd like to get to know
a _____
_____ has _____
_____ wears _____
_____ pet is _____
_____ friends _____
and _____
if I want _____ to
_____

2. Publication of texts.

TEACHER'S QUICK–REFERENCE GUIDE

3.1	Questions	Lower Intermediate +	183
3.2	*What is* + adjective?	Elementary – Lower Intermediate	188
3.3	Questions with *do*	Elementary +	191
3.4	Questions in the third person singular, adverbs of frequency, *taste/smell of*, *feel/look/sound like*	Lower Intermediate +	196
3.5	*Which* as interrogative pronoun	Intermediate +	199
3.6	*Who does it belong to?*	Lower Intermediate +	204
4.1	*If* + present progressive (first conditional), imperatives	Intermediate +	211
4.2	*Whenever*	Lower Intermediate +	215
4.3	*If*– sentences + past perfect (third conditional), statements and *wh*– questions	Intermediate +	220
4.4	Reported speech	Intermediate +	224
4.5	*If*– clause for unreal non–past situations	Intermediate +	228
4.6	Reported commands	Lower Intermediate +	232
4.7	*Could* for possibility and hypothetical ability	Lower Intermediate +	236
4.8	*I wish I* + past	Lower Intermediate +	241
4.9	Reported speech	Intermediate +	245
4.10	*If*– clause + past (second conditional)	Intermediate +	249
4.11	Gerund	Intermediate +	253
4.12	Relative pronouns *who, whose*	Intermediate +	258

Bibliography

Asher, J 1986 *Learning Another Language Through Actions: The Complete Language Teacher's Guidebook* Sky Oaks Productions

Bourke, J M 1989 *The Grammar Gap* English Teaching Forum

Buzan, T 1974 *Use Your Head* Ariel Books, BBC

Davis, P and Rinvolucri, M 1988 *Dictation* CUP

Davis, P and Rinvolucri, M 1990 *The Confidence Book* Longman

Dilts, R B, Epstein, T and Dilts, R W 1991 *Tools for Dreamers: Strategies for Creativity and the Structure of Innovation* Meta Publications

Frank, C and Rinvolucri M, 1987 *Grammar in Action* Prentice Hall

Graham, C 1978 *Jazz Chants* OUP

Graham, C 1979 *Jazz Chants for Children* OUP

Grinder, M 1989 *Righting the Educational Conveyor Belt* Metamorphous Press

Hess, N 1991 *Headstarts* Longman

Houston, J 1982 *The Possible Human* J P Tarcher Inc

Klauser, H A 1986 *Writing on Both Sides of the Brain: Breakthrough Techniques for People Who Write* Harper and Row

Kuskin, K 1980 *Dogs and Dragons, Trees and Dreams* Harper and Row

Landers, A 1968 *Truth is Stranger ...* Prentice Hall

Maley, A and Duff, A 1989 *The Inward Ear* CUP

Mazer, N F 1983 *Someone to Love* Delacorte Press

McGough, R and Rosen, M 1981 *You Tell Me* Puffin Books

Meister Vitale, B 1982 *Unicorns Are Real* Jalmar Press

Mitchell, S 1988 *Tao Te Ching (A New English Version)* Harper and Row

Morgan, J and Rinvolucri, M 1986 *Vocabulary* OUP

Moskowitz, G 1978 *Sharing and Caring in the Foreign Language Classroom* Newbury House

Rinvolucri, M 1984 *Grammar Games* CUP

Rosen, M 1981 *Wouldn't You Like to Know* Puffin Books

Rutherford, W 1987 *Second Language Grammar: Learning and Teaching* Longman

Sachs, M 1987 *The Fat Girl* Corgi Freeway

Stanford, G 1977 *Developing Effective Classroom Groups* Hart Publishing Company

Stevick, E 1996 *Memory, Meaning and Method* (2nd edition) Heinle & Heinle

Stevick, E 1989 *Success With Foreign Languages* Prentice Hall

Swan M, 2005 *Practical English Usage* (3rd edition) OUP

Thornbury, S 2001 *Uncovering Grammar* Macmillan

Thornbury, S 2005 *Grammar* OUP

Ur, P 1988 *Grammar Practice Activities* CUP

Woods, E and McLeod, N 1990 *Using English Grammar: Meaning and Form* Prentice Hall

Wright, A 1984 *1000 Pictures for Teachers to Copy* Collins